C000216148

THE
EIGHTH
SUMMIT

THE EIGHTH SUMMIT

ROW THE ATLANTIC.
RACE TO THE SOUTH POLE.
CONQUER YOURSELF.

PETER van KETS

PETER VAN KETS is a world-renowned adventurer, motivational speaker and conservationist.

He was born in Durban in 1966, and attended a number of schools in both South West Africa (now Namibia) and South Africa. Originally a high- and junior-school teacher, he completed his first Atlantic Rowing Race in 2008 before going on to pursue a career as a full-time adventurer.

Peter has spent a great deal of time in or on the ocean as a diver, surfer, yachtsman and paddler. Kayaking is his major sport, and he has participated in numerous races, including the 255-kilometre Port Elizabeth to East London Surf Ski Challenge. He is a certified Yachtmaster and highly competent navigator, with five ocean crossings by yacht under his belt. He is also an experienced mountain biker and skydiver.

Peter has led and taken part in various expeditions around Africa and the world. His three most high-profile events to date, covered in this book, include twice rowing the Atlantic Ocean and trekking nearly 900 kilometres to the South Pole. Among other accolades, he was honoured as SA OutThere Adventurer of the Year in 2011.

Peter lives in East London with his wife, Kim, also an endurance athlete, and their daughter, Hannah.

Published by Mercury
an imprint of Burnet Media

•

Burnet Media is the publisher of Mercury and Two Dogs books
info@burnetmedia.co.za   www.burnetmedia.co.za
Facebook: Two Dogs / Mercury Books
Twitter: @TwoDogs_Mercury
PO Box 53557, Kenilworth, 7745, South Africa

•

First published 2014
1 3 5 7 9 8 6 4 2

•

Publication © 2014 Burnet Media
Cover photographs courtesy of Shelley Chadburn-Barron and Braam Malherbe
Original maps by Amy Smith

•

All rights reserved. No part of this publication may be reproduced, stored
in a retrieval system or transmitted, in any form or by any means, electronic,
mechanical, photocopying, recording or otherwise, without the prior
written permission of the copyright owners.

•

Distributed by Jacana Media
www.jacana.co.za

•

Printed and bound by Paarl Media
www.paarlmedia.co.za

•

ISBN 9780992194932

For giving me the freedom to dream and for encouraging me to seek out the extraordinary,

This book is dedicated to my beautiful wife, Kim.

Thank you for your unconditional love and support.

You are my greatest gift

Forever.

CONTENTS

FOREWORD
by Professor Tim Noakes

"I'm really just a normal person. I was never a great athlete at school. I didn't win any races or captain any teams. I am tall and skinny and when people meet me they often cannot believe that I have rowed across an ocean (twice!) or trekked 500 miles to the South Pole."

With this analysis Peter van Kets introduces himself and his chosen life career as "adventurer" to us. But it only gets worse. A year before he rowed across the Atlantic for the first time Peter had "never rowed a stroke in my life". Before he went to Antarctica to ski to the South Pole, he had "never cross-country skied – let alone skied in -45°C while pulling almost 100 kilograms on a sledge".

So how does a skinny kid with little athletic ability achieve what others might consider to be impossible? His suggestion described in these pages is that to understand what is possible you must first tackle what you originally conceived to be impossible. And in your search for the impossible you will meet those moments of absolute despair – when disaster seems inevitable. And when you survive that first moment of imminent disaster, and then the next, and the next, it suddenly dawns on you that your concept of the impossible is, well, nothing more than illusion. That it is nothing more than a mental limitation we choose to impose upon ourselves. So it is that when we challenge the impossible we discover, as did Peter, that "the key to success is what happens inside my head". We truly do decide our own destiny. But few understand this. It takes the unconstrained adventurers – people like Peter – to remind us of this truth.

Controlling what is in their heads allowed Peter and his partner Bill Godfrey to row for 90 minutes on, followed by 90 minutes off, for 5,438 kilometres over the course of 50 days 12 hours and 5 minutes in order to win the 2007 Woodvale Atlantic Rowing Race, beating the second boat by less than 30 nautical miles. We learn that their core value was that they were a real team in which each cared more for the other than for himself – in Peter's words: "Our early resolution [was] to each look after the other rower more so than ourselves". Their other key mental strategy, as I told them before they began, was to start the race certain that they would win. For only with that certainty would they be prepared, as Friedrich Nietzsche told us, "to accept any how". And the any how would become the defining statement of who they are – the triumph on which they can now build the rest of their lives.

So this book represents only the beginning of Peter's journey to self-discovery. There is much more to come. The lessons he has learnt coupled with his joy of life, his unfailing enthusiasm and his boundless positivity will continue to drive his eternal quest.

In telling his story, the adventurous skinny boy with little athletic ability has become an inspiration to all of us.

Tim Noakes
April 2014

INTRODUCTION

*"It is not the mountain we conquer
but ourselves."*
– Sir Edmund Hillary

Imagine a scene.

You are in the middle of the Atlantic Ocean in a 7-metre rowing boat. Just you. There are at least 2,000 kilometres of water stretching into the distance on all sides and you could not be more alone.

You have not seen another human being in weeks. You are tired. Your hands are calloused and raw. Your bottom has developed pressure sores on both sides. You have salt sores right where the sun doesn't shine. And, to top it all, you're in a storm with your parachute anchor deployed, a desperate measure to stabilise your puny vessel amid massive ocean swells and battering winds.

It's raining hard and waves are breaking over the boat. You are being tossed around like a cork in a rapid. You are doing your best to lie still in your cabin, which is the size of a coffin – or maybe just a bit bigger. Either way, it feels very much like a coffin to you right now, and the ocean depths beneath you may well be your grave. You really don't know whether you will survive this storm or if the Atlantic will refuse to spit you out on the other side.

Then you notice the laminated print-outs stuck to the roof of the cabin. Some are messages from your wife and pictures of her and your beautiful daughter; others are motivational quotes. One of them catches your attention and it gets you thinking.

> *"Impossible is just a big word thrown around by small men who find it easier to live in the world they've been given than to explore the power they have to change it. Impossible is not a fact. It's an opinion. Impossible is not a declaration. It's a dare. Impossible is potential. Impossible is temporary. Impossible is nothing."*
> – Mohammed Ali

I don't have to imagine this scene; I can vividly recall it. It was January 2010, and I was participating in the Woodvale Atlantic Rowing Race, an unsupported rowing race that covers nearly 5,500 kilometres from the Canary Islands in the east to Antigua Island in the west. The storm in question lasted *six days*...

The moment I have described was, of course, one of great doubt for me – but it was eventually one of great clarity.

Can we really overcome the impossible? Really? Anybody? How do we surmount great obstacles when the odds seem so heavily stacked against us? How do we achieve feats – in all areas of life – when the likelihood of success seems so distant?

I found the answer to all those questions in the middle of the Atlantic Ocean.

My chosen career is "adventurer". To date my three greatest feats are rowing the Woodvale Atlantic twice and trekking to the South Pole.

I completed my first Atlantic crossing in 2007 and early 2008 with a friend, Bill Godfrey. Bill and I rowed in shifts: 90 minutes on and 90 minutes off, 24 hours a day, seven days a week for 50 days and 12 hours. There was not one second on that boat that one of us wasn't rowing except during one particularly bad storm, and for half an hour on Christmas day when we decided to eat our Christmas lunch together and make a satellite call back home to our wives. We endured four radical storms during the race. The final one lasted for four days and we rowed across the finish line as it ended, thoroughly trashed and looking like undernourished prisoners of war. Emerging from the storm and crossing the calm lagoon to the jetty where we were greeted by hundreds of spectators, including South African friends and family who had flown all the way to support us, was one of the greatest highs of my life. We had endured incredible hardship in the pursuit of our dream, which was not only to row across the Atlantic, but to defy all odds and win the race – which we did! On the quayside that evening I promised Kim, my beautiful and long-suffering wife, that I would never do that again…

In 2010 I did it again, but this time I was on my own. I rowed in shifts of 90 minutes on and 90 minutes off, 24 hours a day, 7 days a week – for 76 days. The obvious difference second time around was that whenever I went off shift there was no Bill to take over. One of my biggest challenges was keeping the boat headed in the right direction as much as I could while I rested. Harder than you think.

It's difficult to compare the two rows, but a feature that distinguished the second one from the first was the weather and sea conditions. Besides that one beast of a storm – which endowed me with a real sense of my frailty and smallness in the greater scheme of things – the winds and currents were consistently and frustratingly against me. But as hard and lonely as the row was, it was also a beautiful, life-changing experience.

In January 2012 I took part in a very different type of event. I joined up with Braam Malherbe – known for running the length of the Great Wall of China; more than 4,200 kilometres – and together we formed a two-man South African team to take part in the Centenary Race to the South Pole. First came the 120-kilometre acclimatisation trek, then the 768-kilometre race proper, which together formed an epic 888-kilometre polar odyssey. As a once-off, the Centenary Race was, in my opinion, the toughest endurance event on the planet, not because of its length, but because it is relentlessly dangerous. If you aren't alert enough and quick enough to fix it, just one small mistake at any time during the race can result in the loss of fingers, toes, facial extremities and even your life. In the end, we spent six hostile weeks in the Antarctic wilderness so that we could complete the race.

And yet, for all the painful miles I have travelled and the hardships I've endured, I'm really just a normal person. I was never a great athlete at school. I didn't win any races or captain any teams. I am tall and skinny, and when people meet me they often cannot believe that I have rowed across an ocean (twice!) or trekked 500 miles to the South Pole.

When I signed up to do the race across the Atlantic with Bill, I had never rowed a stroke in my life before. When Braam and I got together to race across Antarctica the coldest temperature I'd experienced was -16°C and I had never cross-country skied – let alone skied in -45°C while pulling almost 100 kilograms on a sledge. People would often tell me I was boxing above my weight. Some thought – and told us – that what we were trying to achieve was impossible and that we were doomed to failure. They were wrong. Bill and I won our race across the Atlantic and Braam and I made it all the way to the South Pole, one of only three teams to do so out of seven that started.

Although I need to be physically fit and strong to do what I do, the key to success is always what happens inside my head. Your body is an incredible thing. It can get used to almost anything and it can go on forever. It's your mind that stops you, that gives up long before your body does.

I experienced a classic example of this during both Atlantic crossings. I was always at my lowest point around 4am. The graveyard shift. I would be absolutely exhausted, slumped over my oars and thinking there was no way I could endure another 24 hours like the previous 24. I would have to really hang in during that shift. But I knew I had something to look forward to that would motivate me during the darkest hours: the five-minute satellite phone call home to my wife Kim that was scheduled afterwards. I would spend the majority of that 4am shift planning my conversation.

Now here's the point. After feeling like I could never survive another day like the previous one, I would speak to Kim, the sun would come up and I would have breakfast. The next shift in daylight, only one-and-a-half hours later, was completely different and I would feel like a new person.

So what's the difference between that time during the last shift when I think I can go on no longer to when I am rowing like a beast again? Physically nothing. The sun has come up, I have made the call home and I have had breakfast, that's all. The change has happened in my head.

I have always marvelled at the nature of the human spirit and at human endeavours. What is it that allows us to endure great hardship in the pursuit of attaining (or not attaining) our seemingly impossible dreams? What am I able to achieve in my life? Do I have limits and, if any, what are they?

The incredible stories of survival and endurance that have been told by explorers such as Ernest Shackleton, Robert Scott and Sir Ranulph Fiennes have always fascinated me. Human endeavour has progressed because of the likes of Columbus and Cook and Livingstone, men who have inspired nations. In recent years South African adventurers such as Mike Horn and Riaan Manser have delivered their own amazing feats. Horn has circumnavigated the equator without the use of motors, climbed the Seven Summits, been to both Poles and beyond. Manser is famed for cycling the entire coastline of Africa, a journey of nearly 37,000 kilometres that took more than two years.

But modern explorers are not as acclaimed as those famous names from the past and, perhaps as a result of this, I believe that men (and women) have forgotten that we have been created with a deep need for adventure, that it is woven deep into our souls, and that the histories of many countries are built on the spirit of adventure. Our modern, stressed (yet physically comfortable) lifestyles have led to a diminishing appetite for physical risk. We no longer see our lives as a grand adventure. But there are great lessons to be learnt in pushing ourselves, physically and mentally, to the edge.

It's this spirit of adventure that drives me in my life. It's what makes me feel alive and what keeps my family vibrant and happy. The very basic core of my living spirit is the passion for adventure, for new experiences. There is no greater joy for me than to have an endlessly changing horizon; for each day to have a new and different sun.

The conclusion that I have come to, having undertaken dozens of endurance adventure expeditions over the years and tested every limit in my body, is that we are able to achieve anything we want – dare I say, "the impossible". It is a conclusion that I held in such sharp relief in that moment in the Atlantic storm in my little rowing boat. There are, however, terms and conditions that apply which create the stumbling blocks for us in life. And more often than not these stumbling blocks, these obstacles, are overcome (or not) inside our heads.

Before the start of every expedition, the thing that energises me the most is the mental test I will have to endure. Will I be able to handle the physical pain, the separation from my beautiful wife and daughter, the loneliness, the fear, the relentlessness of the journey? Will I be able to do all this while at times operating in an animal-like or even subconscious state?

Yes.

The answer is yes because it has to be. But it is also yes because I know how to make it so. In the course of my adventures I have learnt many valuable lessons and in so doing have created a process for my life. It's this process that allows me to dream, to act on my dreams and to achieve them successfully and with significance.

The great dream for many mountaineers is to climb the seven highest mountains across the world's seven continents (as Mike Horn has done) – to conquer the Seven Summits, a remarkable feat. There is, however, one more summit that must be conquered to get there: the Eighth Summit, the personal summit. In other words, you and what happens inside your head.

And so *The Eighth Summit* has very little to do with mountaineering or rock climbing. Rather, it is about the internal expeditions we must all undertake to achieve our goals. This is the essence of what I want to share because I truly believe that if we can master what's happening inside our heads, we can master ourselves – and, in so doing, achieve anything. Then the impossible will, as Mohammed Ali knew, become nothing.

THE WOLF
AND THE DREAM
Leaving a legacy

---

*An old chief passes on words of wisdom to his grandson.
"My boy," he says, "there is a battle between two
wolves inside us all. One is evil. It is anger, jealousy,
greed, fear, resentment, inferiority, lies and ego. The
other is good. It is joy, peace, love, hope, humility,
kindness, empathy and truth."
The boy thought about this for a while and asked,
"Grandfather, which wolf wins?"
The old man quietly replied, "The one you feed."*
– Cherokee legend

For me, one of the hardest parts of any expedition is leaving home. The details may differ slightly from trip to trip, but the thoughts and emotions are essentially the same.

I will never forget reversing out of the driveway of our house on the way to the airport in 2007 to fly out to the Canary Islands for my first *really* big expedition, the Woodvale Atlantic Rowing Race. I live on the east coast of South Africa, just north of East London, in a village called Sunrise-on-Sea. Our home is right on the beach in a nature reserve. It's a beautiful place. As I reversed my bakkie out of the driveway I paused for a moment. Kim was sitting next to me and my daughter Hannah was in the back, strapped into her car seat. I looked at my family, our home, the garden, and drank them all in. Two things went through my mind.

The first thought, a fleeting one, I kept to myself. I wondered if I would ever see my home and family or this beautiful place again. I was about to venture into the unknown, on an expedition that entails a very real element of risk. But the dangers had been weighed and the decisions made many months before. There was no point in dwelling on doubts or fears. According to Cherokee wisdom, there is an ongoing battle within our minds between two wolves, one representing the good in us, the other the bad. We need to be mindful, disciplined and resolute to steer clear of the negative emotions that feed the bad wolf. So I quickly put aside my fear.

I was more open to my second thought. Feeling a surge of excitement and expectation, I turned to Kim. "Isn't this the most amazing thing?" I said. "In three months' time, the very next time we drive back into this driveway together, there is going to be a story that needs to be told... and I wonder what that story's going to be?"

I knew that the story would be filled with hardships beyond my best planning, and that I was going to be tested physically, emotionally and spiritually beyond the limits of my imagination. That is the nature of extreme expeditions. I knew, too, that I would experience incredible things. Rowing across a vast blue ocean and interacting with nature in a true wilderness would be a privilege. The sunrises and sunsets. The squalls and storms. The victories and failures. I couldn't wait for the anticipation to be over and the story to begin.

Together, Kim and I chose to focus on these positive thoughts as we drove towards the airport (and the dreaded goodbyes). We consciously chose to feed the good wolf.

Months later, when I returned home, there was indeed a story to tell – and there would be more to come in my subsequent adventures. Some of these stories are contained within these pages, and others are yet to be written. But all stories start with a dream. *The Eighth Summit* itself began as a dream – to write a book. Without the dream, the critical part of any story, we will never have a significant tale to tell one day.

As you read this book I would like you to think about your own life story. What is the story you will tell your friends and your grandchildren one day? What is the legacy that you wish to leave behind you? Is it one of daring, of making a difference, of success? And, most importantly, is it one of significance? (There is a great difference between significance and success.) How do we ensure that the story we will tell one day is one of both success *and* significance?

In my opinion, to be "successful" without being significant means nothing. We strive so hard to become successful that it is easy to lose sight of one of the most important parts of our lives: purpose. To me, a significant person is someone who lives his or her life with purpose – or meaning or consequence, if you prefer – and who has a positive effect on other people. If you were to go to sleep tonight and not wake up in the morning, would you have left this planet a better place? Would there be at least one person who is breathing easier because of what you have done for him or her?

If you had to fast-forward your life by a year, or perhaps a decade, do you think you'd have a compelling story to tell at the end of that time? Do you wonder about your story?

While life is full of the mystery of the unexpected, with no guarantees for even the best-laid plans, I believe there is a path to success and significance, and I have put a process in place in my life to try to achieve them both. Each of the chapters of this book has a key to unlock that process, and the first, critically important key is our ability to dream.

As we get older we lose that ability to dream. It's a sad fact of life. We get caught up in our work and careers. The stresses of finance and relationships and keeping it all together evolve into a full-time occupation. We become "sensible". It's for this reason that we put our dreams "on hold" – or we simply stop dreaming altogether. The dreams that used to fuel us and inspire us eventually vanish.

(Young people are brilliant at dreaming. Once when she was four years old, I asked my daughter what she dreamed of doing with her life one day. She replied with absolute certainty, "Dad, I want to be an extreme rock-climbing ballerina!" I'm not at all sure that there is such a thing – although why not? – but I was very happy to know she was dreaming about her future.)

Our *dreams* are always linked to our *passions,* which point us in the direction of our *purpose.* What is it that makes you come alive? When did you last feel that thrill of excitement and creativity, those butterflies in your stomach, an involuntary smile on your face, the feeling that time has absolutely flown by as you've been swept up in something that really switches you on?

Each and every one of us is wired differently. It could be any number of things that energises your soul: writing a book or travelling or playing a musical instrument or painting or surfing or cooking a gourmet meal or solving a complex set of problems... I'm a firm believer that God has planted a deep desire and passion for *something* in all of our hearts.

Sadly, many sensible adults have forgotten what recharges their batteries and makes them feel most alive. Or, worse still, they think it's shopping or watching sport on TV or their first drink of the day. As the great theologian and Nobel Prize winner Albert Schweitzer put it, "The tragedy of life is what dies inside a person while they still live."

When we make the big decisions about how we spend our time and resources, it is so important that we ask ourselves what makes us come alive (rather than what is sensible or secure or expected of us). And then we need to go out into the world and devote our time to doing exactly that, because what the world needs more than anything are vital, passionate men and women doing what they were created to do – men and women who have truly come alive.

We don't all have the privilege of making our passions our livelihood, but that is no excuse to give them up. It is our duty to rediscover these passions and use them to recharge our batteries and fulfil our purpose and, in so doing, help others whenever we can. There is something about tapping into your passion regularly that makes the rest of your life fall into place. Our passions are always a clue to our dreams and ultimately our real purpose.

I hope that my story will challenge you to feed your good wolf, to dream and to rediscover that thing that makes you feel most alive. It has been planted inside you for a purpose. Let's not just climb the ordinary mountains. Let's seek out the extraordinary ones and conquer them with significance.

PART I

THE LION ROARS

First undertaken in 1997, and subsequently held every two years, the Atlantic Rowing Race is without doubt one of the most daunting races of any kind in the world. In rowing boats measuring just seven by two metres, competitors inch their way from the Canary Islands off the west coast of Africa to the island of Antigua in the Caribbean Sea, a distance of nearly 5,500 kilometres. In 2007 I was given the opportunity to compete with Bill Godfrey in what was then the Woodvale Atlantic Rowing Race (now the Talisker Whisky Atlantic Challenge). It was an event that changed my life.

GQUMA CHALLENGER VERSUS THE ATLANTIC OCEAN

"Peter van Kets and Bill Godfrey overcame the limitations of their minds and so achieved an historic victory for themselves and their nation."
– **Professor Tim Noakes**

The story of *Gquma Challenger* begins in 2005 and ends with a promise I was not to keep.

It was a chance meeting that changed the course of my life forever. Appropriately, given my love of the ocean and the adventure to follow, it happened while heading out to surf at Queensberry Bay, just north of East London. Queensberry, a favourite surf spot of mine, is one of the most idyllic point breaks along the South African coastline, an isolated bay with generally relaxed and friendly surfers. It's not uncommon for locals to offer the next wave to newcomers, something unheard of at 99 percent of the world's surf spots. As a regular, I recognised familiar faces behind the breakers, including, when a friend introduced us while we were paddling out together, Bill Godfrey's. The introduction went something like this.

"Pete, this is Bill. Bill wants to row across the Atlantic Ocean. Bill, this is Pete. Pete is planning to paddle unsupported in sea kayaks from South Africa to Madagascar. You two have a lot to talk about." And off our mutual friend paddled, leaving Bill and me sitting on our boards and chatting about the different expeditions we were thinking about. I was indeed considering an unsupported kayaking expedition across the Mozambique Channel to Madagascar, a trip I would have to place on the bucket list for the time being, as Bill's plan to compete in the 2007 Woodvale Atlantic Rowing Race seemed far more exciting.

Our chance meeting quickly turned to deep conversation. I sensed that Bill was very serious about the race and was determined to make it work. As a one-time member of the South African national rowing squad, he had serious credentials. At that stage, however, he had almost exhausted his sponsorship contacts and things were not looking good. A friend, Dave Pattle, who had been interested in rowing with him, had been forced to pull out because of family commitments, and he had reached a point requiring new energy and some positive input. Suddenly he had a likely candidate bobbing in the waves next to him. Though I was not a rower, I was always game for an adventure and I had a reasonable amount of ocean-going experience. I had twice contested the 250-kilometre Port Elizabeth to East London Surf Ski Challenge, I had undertaken a couple of ocean crossings by yacht, and I was the proud owner of a Yachtmaster Offshore Certificate, which allowed me to skipper a boat across any ocean.

Before we paddled our separate ways into the surf, Bill asked me if I would like to take his friend's place and be his rowing partner. At the time Kim was barely two months away from giving birth to our daughter Hannah, and there was no way I was going home to tell my pregnant wife I'd decided, while surfing, to flit off and row across the Atlantic for a few months. Needless to say, she would have pulled out the shotgun. So my life-preserving response was something along the lines of, "No, but call me again in a few months if you haven't found anyone else. Once Hannah is born things may have settled."

Almost to the day six months later I received a call from Bill. He hadn't had any luck finding a partner. Amazingly, he sounded slightly surprised that no-one was keen. Funny thing, that!

By this stage I had almost forgotten our conversation behind the breakers at Queensberry Bay, but when I heard his voice again my heart skipped a beat. Hannah was a few months old and the post-pregnancy dust had almost settled. There may be a chance that this epic row could actually happen…

At first Bill told me he was just calling for advice. He had decided to row the race solo, he said, and wanted to know if

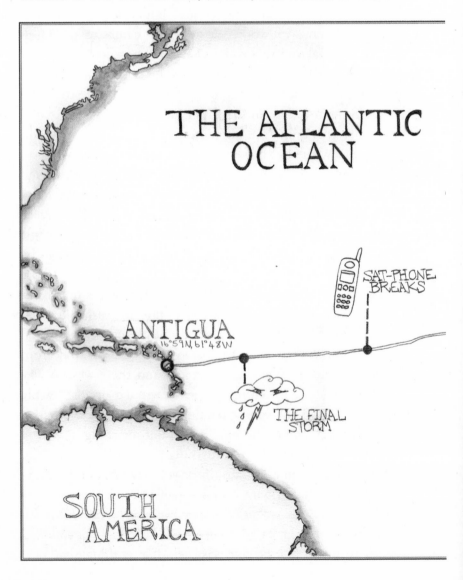

I could assist him on the navigational side of things, given my experience. I explained how the North Atlantic high-pressure system worked and how that might affect his route decision. At the end of the conversation he finally came out with the real reason for the call: he wanted me to race with him.

With a new addition to the family, my decision could only be made with input from Kim. The two of us have an incredibly

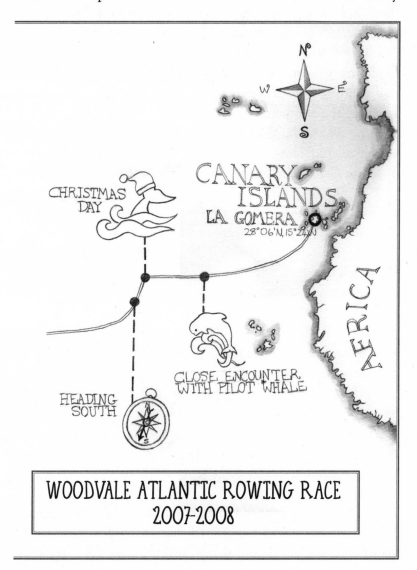

CHRISTMAS DAY

CANARY ISLANDS
LA GOMERA
28°06'N, 15°24'W

AFRICA

CLOSE ENCOUNTER WITH PILOT WHALE

HEADING SOUTH

WOODVALE ATLANTIC ROWING RACE 2007-2008

strong relationship, which works on the mutual understanding that we share the responsibilities of our marriage equally. For something as big as this there would need to be a serious discussion, and it would largely depend on how she felt spending so much time apart and without my help. As a legal advisor for Mercedes Benz, she had her career to consider, and she would have to work and hold the fort at home while I was away. Beyond that, there was the danger factor. The race would be entirely unsupported and a lot can go wrong in a 5,000-kilometre expanse of water. At the same time, Kim is herself an active, outdoorsy person, and would go on to become something of a trail-running legend, eventually running, mountain biking and kayaking the perimeter of South Africa. It was a tough call.

In the end, it came down to a bunch of flowers and a copy of the documentary *Though Hell And High Water*, the story of James Cracknell and Ben Fogle's race across the Atlantic in 2005. I picked up the latter from Bill's office in East London and bought the former on the way home, before sitting down with Kim to explain the opportunity to her. After talking about it in some depth and then watching the documentary, she turned to me with an expression I will never forget, and said, "Pete, if this is your dream, I will never stop you. Go for it!"

Kim: Being cast in the supporting role of the anxious wife is by comparison decidedly unglamorous – especially seeing as I have always fantasised about being the Gladiator character rather than his girlfriend! But the supporting role is critical and it has its own special set of skills. I needed to hone those skills to allow Peter to achieve his dream.

The race was on. I called Bill and told him the news, but before I went into any detail I explained that I would commit to the venture on one condition: that during the race his focus must be on me and my focus must be on him. In other words, we would look after each other more so than ourselves. If I became dehydrated, he would make sure I drank more. If he started feeling depressed and miserable – as happens on expeditions of this nature – it was my job to lift his spirits, and vice versa. Though I was still an amateur adventurer, I had had enough wilderness experiences to realise that people tend to withdraw into their own world and then only focus on themselves after a few days out of their comfort zone, ultimately creating dangerous situations that can lead to conflict.

Of course I was aware I was committing to a major undertaking, but I could not have known the many twists and turns (and forks and dead ends and amazing opportunities) the path I had just started on would present. It was the beginning of a new journey for me, one that continues today. I had no idea how my life was about to change.

Bill and I committed to taking part in the 2007 Woodvale Atlantic Rowing Race together in November 2005. It was the start of more than two years of intense training, extended periods away from home, trips around the country in search of sponsors and to complete the various requisite courses we needed to enter the race, more training and massive financial stress. I found the Survival at Sea, First Aid at Sea and Yachtmaster Ocean Celestial Navigation courses all relatively easy going, but each cost money and the expenses mounted. Sponsor after potential sponsor emailed variations on the following theme: "We regret to inform you that, while the idea of rowing across an ocean may fill you with enthusiasm, it holds no similar appeal for our marketing department who advise that any available funds may be better spent on obtaining psychiatric intervention. Nevertheless best of luck in your misdirected endeavour, etc etc."

Despite the negative responses, we kept at it every day, contacting more and more people, requesting financial support or seeking out technical advice and assistance. From the beginning we decided that if we were going to do this thing, we may as well do it properly – that is, we should aim to win it. We spoke to Professor Tim Noakes at the Sports Science Institute of South Africa, and he assisted with our physical training programme and mental approach.

There was some humour along the way. When Bill and I took part in the Survival at Sea course, the class was populated largely by non-swimming Nigerian oil-rig workers, whose employment depended on their passing this course… Survival at Sea pretty much turned into the real thing as Bill and I spent the entire swimming phase darting around the pool rescuing terrified, semi-drowned Nigerians. When the instructor asked us to "pick a partner", half the class launched themselves at Bill and the other half went for me!

In time, we started building up a support team. Kim and Kate, Bill's wife, were the heart; we would have got nowhere without their unqualified backing. On Prof Noakes's advice, I made contact with the wonderful and interesting David Becker, who was living in Dubai at the time, employed at the International Cricket Council headquarters. He agreed to be our mind coach, a role he performed for many years for his friend Lewis Pugh, the world-renowned polar swimmer. My old friend Nic Good, otherwise known as Moose, was also a pillar of moral support as well as our filmmaker. Owner of Fresh Air Crew, a film company that specialises in making adventure documentaries, he was in charge of putting together a documentary for SuperSport. Tjaart van der Walt, our weatherman, was another long-time friend. He would become the crucial point of contact when we checked in from the boat by satellite phone, helping to guide us across the ocean. (Tjaart, pronounced Chart, was, I thought, an appropriate name for a weatherman.)

The final key piece in the puzzle was not human, but a character nevertheless: our boat, christened *Gquma Challenger*, an onomatopoeic Xhosa word representing the roar of a lion or the sound of crashing waves. Measuring 7.1 by 1.9 metres, she would carry all our food and equipment for two months at sea.

Her layout was simple enough. At the stern was the cabin, our shared bedroom that was barely long enough for a man to lie down flat without his feet sticking out the hatch. The cabin contained the all-important communication equipment and navigational instruments. Amidships came the two rowing positions. Most of the time there would only ever be one person on the oars, though there would be occasions when we rowed together. Towards the bow was the storage compartment for the parachute anchor and drogues, rope, anchor and the like. Solar panels were affixed to various surfaces to charge two deep-cycle batteries that would power the radio, desalinator for making drinking water and GPS.

In the build-up to the start of the race, sponsorship was proving to be our biggest obstacle. But it's remarkable how, once you've committed to something, these things tend to work out in the end. A healthy dose of faith is often required to realise a grand dream or vision. Knowledge and ideas aren't enough; as the megabrand Nike knows so well, eventually you must *just do it* to get it done. Or, if you prefer the (slightly misquoted) wisdom of the baseball classic *Field of Dreams*, "If you build it, they will come." It's a self-fulfilling prophecy that has resurfaced so many times during the course of my adventuring career.

Bill had decided to invest in an ocean rowing boat that he would import from the UK and sell after the event, hopefully for more than the purchase price (because it would have won a race!). He had a contact at an international logistics company, DB Schenker, who agreed to cover the forward and clearing costs. We figured that once the boat was landed in South Africa we would have a better chance of securing sponsors.

The day *Gquma Challenger* arrived at the DB Schenker facility in East London, the company CEO, Tony Pheiffer, was coincidentally visiting. He had not heard of our row yet but was fascinated by it, and was delighted his company had been of some assistance to us. "Is there anything else you need assistance with?" he then asked.

"Now that's a question we've been waiting to hear for a

long time," I replied. As we rolled the boat out he phoned his counterparts in Germany and they agreed there and then to sponsor all our shipping and to throw in €2,000.

Things were looking up. I then met with Ian Gallacher of Garmin Africa, who was particularly interested our race; he agreed to personally sponsor all our navigational equipment. Ian would go on to be a great moral and financial support for my subsequent crossing too. It was a good start, but we still had the race entry fee to pay and time was running out.

I have a very close relationship with a few of my uncles, and being old "sea dogs" they, too, were taken by the idea of the row. One morning I received a call from one, John Donnelly, to find out how the preparations were going. We eventually got on to the race entry fee and our deadlines. To my amazement, he called back a few hours later with the news that he and his brother Lionel had agreed to pay the fee. I was completely thrown. I'm not one for involving family and money, so I was a bit hesitant, but they won me over with their generosity. It was the most generous gift I could have ever imagined, and without my uncles I'm not sure the story would have had such a happy ending.

We still needed a further $30,000 to cover the remaining costs. As fate would have it, the money eventually came from the company that built the aluminium mounting for our cooker. I called a friend, Brian Harmse, who owned the East London businesses TFM and Fabkomp to ask about the mounting, and we got chatting. A day later he called back to say he would like to be our title sponsor for the race and could I please send our banking details. Unbelievable! The money was deposited the same day, and we were all set for the race of our lives.

Despite overwhelming odds and countless logistical challenges, we made it to the starting line in San Sebastián on the island of La Gomera as the only African entry in the 2007 Woodvale Atlantic Rowing Race. Even then, it was only just. We had a mandatory two weeks on the island to prepare our boats for close scrutiny by race officials – the scrutineers – but our final preparations were hampered dramatically by the fact that our boat failed to make it through customs until five days before the start. It was a huge relief when we finally got it down to the quay. Now we just had an ocean to row across...

Together with 22 other entrants, we finally got under way at midday on 2 December 2007. As the sound of the starting siren floated away in the briny spray, we heard Bill's dad shout "Gooooo Bokke!"– we were off! We headed for the horizon and into the unknown, with a physical challenge of epic proportions before us and without the prospect of seeing land again for two months. As the competing boats disappeared from view one by one, we found ourselves on our own, surrounded by ocean, a frightening and exhilarating realisation. This was it.

Bill and I had spent a lot of time discussing the critical issue of how long our rowing shifts should be. The best advice we could find came from those who had done the race before, and we eventually came to the conclusion that two hours on and two hours off was the accepted routine for a competitive team. That was what we'd trained for and that's how we began – but of course the best-laid plans often go astray.

Within hours the weather turned. It started to rain and the wind changed direction, whipping the sea into a heaving mess. Bill began feeling nauseous.

Seasickness had been the demise of many a team in previous races, and is a far deadlier challenge than non-seafarers may realise. As the author of *Surviving The Extremes*, Kenneth Kamler, describes it, "*Nautical* and *nausea* share the same Greek root. Seasick sailors spend the first half of their voyage afraid they are going to die and the second half hoping they will." Seasickness can be so debilitating over an extended period that it literally saps the will to live, and is considered, after exposure, to be one of the greatest threats to castaways, especially in the first few days after a ship has gone down. Sufferers may not be able to perform basic tasks such as navigating, communicating or keeping their raft seaworthy, which can lead to their downfall long before thirst and starvation kick in. For us the problem was competitive; you simply cannot row if you have been constantly sick over an extended period because the act of vomiting steadily decreases your energy supply while increasing your energy demands.

Bill toughed it out as best he could, powering through his shifts despite all the vomiting, but it quickly became a worry for us. Depending on the severity, three days is about as much seasickness as a man can take while exerting himself physically.

We had to rethink our shift structure. Two hours was just too long for Bill to row while repeatedly vomiting, particularly because he would quickly recover when he stopped and rested, so we shortened our shifts to one hour on and one hour off. The change made a difference, but it was still tough going.

By the third morning of the trip, I was really concerned about Bill. There is only so much you can vomit without becoming severely dehydrated. I told him that today was the day we had to sort out his seasickness. If he wasn't better by that evening we would have to pull the plug on the campaign. I think this brought home the reality of our situation to Bill, as after his shift he immediately disappeared into the cabin and took a suppository of some description. It worked; by that evening he had almost totally recovered. We had already lost a fair bit of distance to the race leaders, but now we could get going properly.

The next day we discussed our rowing routine again and, needing more rest between shifts, decided to change it back to two hours on, two hours off. Then, after a few two-hour sessions we changed again, this time to 90-minute shifts. We had hit on the routine that worked for us, and we stuck to it for the rest of the race, covering an average of 2.5 nautical miles (4.5 kilometres) per hour and 58 nautical miles (108 kilometres) a day.

Our new-found rhythm allowed us to power back into the race, and over the next few days we managed to haul in the leaders. Over the course of the two weeks we had spent in San Sebastián we had tried to establish who our prime competition would be.

Now we could see that it was the boys in *Pendovey Swift*, *No Fear* and *Go Commando* who were pushing the hardest.

For the next seven weeks, spanning Christmas and taking us into a new year, 2008, we were tested physically and emotionally far beyond any point we could have trained for. My relationship with Bill was pushed to the limit but never faltered as we lived together in the intimate confines of a seven-metre wooden boat.

While one of us rowed, the other spent his 90 minutes of down time preparing food and hydration, navigating, performing (very basic) ablutions and attempting to rest in the tiny cabin. Other duties included lubricating the wheel bearings of the seat wheels to keep our oar stroke as smooth as possible; checking equipment and making repairs; washing our rowing clothes, as cleanliness was vital to try to prevent salt-water sores; cleaning and tidying the deck and cabin; and filming for the video diary. Once a day we would check in by sat-phone with Kim, Kate and Tjaart for race and weather updates and emotional support. This may not sound like the longest list, but even simple-sounding tasks are harder than you might imagine when undertaken after little or no sleep on a constantly pitching and heaving platform with ever-decreasing energy levels.

A more high-maintenance task was the cleaning of *Gquma*'s hull, which we took in turns. Cleaning barnacles off your boat's hull is a perhaps surprising duty to add to the chores list on a trans-Atlantic boat crossing. After all, how much barnacle growth can accumulate on the hull of a small rowing boat over the course of a couple of months, and how much can it slow you down? Turns out, a lot (even over a thick coating of anti-fouling paint) and significantly – certainly enough to justify the half-hour cleaning process every four or five days.

Sailors of old were so astounded by barnacle growth that they believed they spontaneously generated from the hull itself. Today we know that barnacle larvae float freely in ocean water waiting for a hard surface to which they can attach themselves, their prevalence and growth rate depending on a number of factors, such as water temperature, light, salinity and current flow. In the tropical waters through which we rowed they are abundant and fast-growing, particularly goose or stalked barnacles, which resemble a white mussel on a stalk after a few days' growth. Every additional barnacle that attaches to your boat adds weight and reduces the streamline of the hull. We soon discovered that the problem was exacerbated at night when the barnacles opened up to filter feed, creating even more drag in the process. In unfavourable conditions when hull cleaning is impossible you might go a week without giving your hull a scrub; when you finally dive overboard and scrape off the accumulated growth you can increase your speed up to 0.5 knots, a huge psychological boost.

There was barely a moment during our 50 days that one of us wasn't rowing, except on one occasion when conditions were utterly hopeless and the parachute anchor was deployed, and on Christmas day when we took 30 minutes off to share a Christmas lunch and call home to talk to our families.

Kim: I had always been grateful that I am the partner who got to endure childbirth, rather than having to watch helplessly while Peter did so – but it certainly seemed that the tables had been turned in those 50 days! I can think of no other way to describe it other than to say that it was much like knowing that Peter was going through a massively complicated, painful and lengthy labour somewhere on the other side of the globe and that I was powerless to do anything to assist other than to keep the home fires burning and the bills paid, and to send a barrage of positive, entertaining and motivational phone calls, SMSes and emails.

My job was to manage the home front in Pete's absence and not to confront him with problems that he was powerless to solve from a distance. No point in telling him I had found a snake under the fridge, that I had a flat tyre and couldn't reconnect the gas on my first attempt. No point in telling him I hadn't exercised for a week because I was too exhausted and grumpy or because I had no-one to take care of Hannah. This wasn't easy!

After a couple of days of wallowing in self-pity it dawned on me that self-pity is the most disempowering and unhelpful emotion, and that it was critical for both of us that I focus on the positive, maintain a sense of humour and stop acting like a poor victim of my unfortunate circumstances. So instead of lying in the foetal position on the couch, I put Hannah in her three-wheeler off-road pram and took her for a 10km run. What a breakthrough!

Now that I had stopped feeling sorry for myself my sense of humour returned and I was able to motivate Pete. Sure you have bleeding hands and aching glutes, BUT you're missing Eskom load shedding, the Zuma election debacle, crowded Christmas shopping centres, fighting for parking at the local Spar... And oh my word, it's going to be worth it when you get your butt to Antigua!

I missed Kim and Hannah, and in the early hours of every morning I pined for them. In these moments it was easy to get down. A major task for Bill and me was to keep each other's spirits up and avoid confrontations. A small problem at home is easy to deal with, but take someone out of his comfort zone and put him in a completely isolated and vulnerable situation where he's suffering from sleep deprivation, boils on the bum and a variety of other physical complaints, and that normally small problem can become all too much to deal with.

Our hands, in particular, suffered terribly, showing signs of fatigue early in the race. We were wet a lot of the time, and the hard black callouses we had worked so hard on developing during training quickly turned soft and white. The gloves we had opted to use seemed to make no difference, and I could feel new blisters being formed under the old skin. I tried to ignore the problem, hoping that it would settle, but it was simply the first of many.

The blister-callous-blister cycle was something we both got used to, but I found the chafe from folds in the leather gloves debilitating. Once it took hold properly, every stroke for the first 15 minutes of every shift was pure agony. Even worse was the tendonitis that I developed as the race progressed. As I rested after a shift, my hands would get stiffer and stiffer and it became increasingly difficult to close them around the oar on the following shift. At first I would simply row through the pain until my hands were warm and the problem disappeared. Later I had to strap my hands in position when I was off shift. I would bind my four fingers to the palm of my hand with a piece of bandage then, using my unstrapped thumbs, would release the bandages before I went back on deck to row again.

Despite the constant physical deterioration, we endured without incident. A major blowout can break a campaign, but we were lucky not to suffer one. I can honestly say that over the course of the entire race we suffered only one minor disagreement – and that was on New Year's Eve when we couldn't decide whether we should use the video camera's infrared light or a headlamp to film our New Year's messages...

Our early resolution to each look after the other rower more so than ourselves paid off. Bill was my project, and I was his. We objectively monitored each other's food, drink and health, a process that allowed us to take our minds off our own suffering and focus on something else for a while. Equally importantly, we constantly motivated each other, as we had done throughout our training, and we did our best to find new ways to do it.

For me, the most difficult aspects in a day's rowing – other than the excruciating 3am shift, which was a real killer – was waking up and getting ready for the next shift. In time we worked out a strict wake-up process, which became a motivating and amusing part of our journey. Ten minutes before the end of his shift the rower would wake up the non-rower so that he could prepare for his session, organising a quick snack and getting his hands ready. If it was night-time, the non-rower would put on something warm and organise his headlamps. During the day, he would apply sunblock and put on his hat.

As the race wore on and every microsecond of sleep became more and more vital, that ten-minute wake-up call became increasingly accurate. In the last few weeks it was probably the closest to-the-second wake-up call ever. With our bodies aching all over and screaming for more rest, it became excruciatingly difficult to get up and we had to find a way to make it easier. So we came up with a simple solution that would make us happy to be awake – sort of. Now, instead of just calling to each other, the wake-up routine went something like this.

"Bill!' I would shout. Then, once I had heard a definite sign of wakefulness, I would shout again. "You won't believe it, bru, but we are 90 MINUTES CLOSER TO ANTIGUA!"

In return, he would reply, "YAHOOOOO!"

Try to picture the scene. It's the middle of the night, you're beyond exhausted and you're being tossed around in your cabin unsuccessfully trying to sleep. Then you hear your rowing partner shout your name, followed up with, "You won't believe it, bru, but we are 90 minutes closer to Antigua!" And through your misery you have to shout, "Yahoo!"

Very odd, but it made me laugh many times. And it worked wonders. I really believe that this type of attitude towards the race was one of the reasons why we did so well in the end.

It's hard to describe what it's like enduring a mid-ocean storm in a small boat. We liked to use the phrase "like a cork in a rapid" to describe the physical effect, but the emotional tumble dryer is something else. When you're off-shift and you're cloistered in the coffin-sized cabin on your own, the combination of discomfort, claustrophobia and relentlessness is almost overwhelming. When you're on the oars, it verges from moment to moment between exhilarating and terrifying.

Bill and I had to survive four storms together. The last two, late in the race, were the most noteworthy for different reasons.

The third storm came days after continuous heavy winds from the northeast, which built up the sea into huge swells capped with white horses breaking on their crests. These were easily big enough to swallow your whole boat for a few moments. It got especially frightening at night when our visibility was reduced to nothing by the darkness and rain swirling into our eyes. We had to rely on our senses and sea knowledge to anticipate when dangerous waves were coming. Listening was the easiest way.

One such evening while I was in the cabin trying to rest, I heard a massive wave breaking over the boat. It thundered over us with a loud bang and I could feel we had spent some time submerged. In those split seconds I was tremendously worried about Bill being washed overboard, even though he was firmly attached to the boat with a leash. As soon as I could, I opened the hatch to find him lying on the deck with a look of the gravest concern in his eyes. No doubt I would have sported a similar look if it were me lying there. After checking the deck for loose or missing items I returned to the cabin, somewhat concerned about my next shift. The sea was roaring.

The next 90 minutes of my life were a roller coaster of excitement and insanity. With waves continuously breaking over the stern of the boat, we surfed down mighty swells as the noise of the sea thundered around us. It made for one epic adrenaline session. Each time the boat pitched and caught a swell it would shudder as it screamed down the wall. It was an ongoing battle to keep us going straight so we wouldn't pitch sideways across the breaking wave. A roll under those conditions would have been extremely dangerous; something to avoid at all costs, which we managed by the narrowest of margins on numerous occasions.

The raging seas calmed after three days, and with the storm behind us we were able to concentrate again on our rowing speed and navigation strategy. We were in first position, but only just! With 600 nautical miles to go, our closest rival was *No Fear*, only 30 nautical miles behind us, leaving us with very little room for error.

Round about this time, our satellite phone started giving us trouble. It struggled to charge for a day or two, and then all of a sudden it stopped working. This meant absolutely no communication with the outside world. No weather updates, no race information, no chats with our wives and children. We were devastated. To compound things, it happened on the same day our families arrived in Antigua.

We had to get over the setback though. We had another ten days at sea to survive and we had to focus on the task at hand.

Kim: Going to meet Peter in Antigua was not quite as glamorous as one would imagine. The romance of such a holiday pales somewhat when it is preceded by a very long flight with multiple transfers alone with a toddler. Also, from examining the post-race state of previous competitors, I anticipated that my usually gorgeous husband would be reduced to a prisoner-of-war lookalike with fungal infections blighting his nether regions – not exactly my partner of choice for a romantic Caribbean holiday!

When we reached the island we received reports of yachts being struck by lightning in the safety of English Harbour. Not a comforting thought when your husband is clutching a set of carbon oars in the middle of the ocean. To make matters worse, we now had no way of communicating with the boat. The wait was agonising.

Four days before we reached Antigua and quite out of the blue, as we now had no weather reports to assist us, the final storm hit. The afternoon before, the sea started its usual storm dance and the grey skies began to close in on us. It was not what we wanted at this stage of the race. With our slim lead, we had hoped for a clear run to the finish line – not a spanner in the works that could allow *No Fear* to slip past us at the death. But perhaps our broken sat-phone was a blessing in disguise. Had we known the enormity of the storm that was about to hit us, we may have been even more concerned. We were tired and we just wanted the race to be over – we were just so close…

If you have ever been close to lightning you will know the tremendous noise that it makes. Sitting in a seven-metre rowing boat holding four-metre carbon oars is not ideal in such circumstances. The roar of the sea mixed with continuous lightning blasts was deafening. There were times in the next few days that the wind would exceed 120km/h and the driving rain would make it unbearable to open our eyes. We could not see our compass, barely two metres in front of us. We could not sleep. Not for a second in four days. We rode massive swells and were battered by waves that threw us across the boat. At one stage our Emergency Position Indicating Radio Beacon, or EPIRB, was activated by a wave and for several hours we were the target of an international rescue operation. By the end of the storm's third day, Day 49 on the ocean, both of us were hallucinating, seeing weird visions and constantly hearing voices.

It was not all doom and gloom, though, as by that point we had only 58 nautical miles to go. Just one more day. And when that final day arrived, the storm had broken and the weather began to ease off. We spotted patches of blue sky here and there and the waves started to subside along with the wind. We also noticed how the shape of the swells and the way they broke at the crest started to change, which indicated shallower depths as we approached land.

That afternoon, while on shift, I heard a noise and I strained my eyes to find its source. Then I saw it. A helicopter zig-zagging across the ocean as though looking for something. Then it disappeared. Bill told me I was hallucinating again and that it was most likely a bird. Five minutes later it returned and this time it came straight at us. Not a bird, this was a helicopter and it was definitely looking for us. We jumped around the boat trying to find something bright to attract their attention. I waved my red Cape Storm rain jacket and Bill waved the South African flag.

Next thing they were hovering above us, and inside we could make out Kim, Kate and Moose, our trusty cameraman, looking down. They were so close we could see the expressions on their faces; they were all crying, even Moose and the helicopter pilot. They had lived through the storm on the island and were simply relieved we had made it through in one piece. Bill and I shouted and screamed and hugged each other in delight.

Not knowing whether we were still in first position or not, I looked up at Moose, who was half dangling out the helicopter, and I pointed my index finger in the air to ask if we were still in first position. His reply was the same an umpire gives to someone who goes out. Yes, we were still first. What a feeling!

Kim: Seeing Peter for the first time in two months was an indescribable experience. I was terrified of what we were going to find, as we had no idea what shape they were going to be in. We worried one of them might be injured.

We had their coordinates and we flew in massive circles over their position – completely invisible to us. The white horses were substantially bigger than the boat. Eventually we spotted them waving their red foul-weather gear, and circled so low that we could make eye contact. In that moment I knew they were okay. It was only from the air that I fully grasped how massively vulnerable and isolated they had been for so long.

The sun was setting by the time they left, and we were buzzing with excitement, the island now clearly visible. We spotted the lights of yachts coming out to greet us, and the excitement was almost too much for us to bear. So close, yet still another seven hours of rowing.

It was a profoundly emotional moment when at 9.05pm on 22 January 2008, after 50 days at sea, we crossed the finish line off Shirley Point near English Harbour, Antigua, securing the Pairs Trophy in the Atlantic Rowing Race for South Africa for the first time. A substantial crowd lined the dock as we emerged from the inky blackness beyond the harbour brandishing the South

African flag and punching the air in victory. As we made our way between all the anchored yachts in the harbour, the local yachties all came out on their decks blowing horns, shouting greetings and setting off handheld flares. It was a sight to remember! Hundreds of people lined the quayside and the South Africans among them sang *Nkosi Sikelel' iAfrika*, our national anthem. What a moment!

It was over. We had done it.

Finally moored in English Harbour, our GPS registered 5,438 kilometres covered – all rowed. The race had been an incredible ultra-marathon, testing both of us to the limit physically, emotionally and spiritually. Having faced serious life-threatening odds, including violent storms, horrific blisters and claw grip, debilitating fatigue, salt and pressure sores, dehydration, heat exhaustion, sunburn and seasickness, we had overcome extreme hardship to accomplish our dream.

I looked across at Bill. He stood up and I put my hands on his shoulders. We hugged each other for the last time on that boat and stepped onto dry land after 50 days, 12 hours and 5 minutes at sea.

I was dizzy from not having slept for the past four days and from the excitement of arriving and seeing Kim and Hannah. It was a sensory overload. I could barely stand upright as I took my first few steps on the hard, firm quayside. I will never forget my first words to Kim after stepping off the boat. I buried my head into her neck and said, "Never, never, never again! I promise never to put you through this again. If I ever tell you some time in the future that I want to row an ocean again please don't let me, as I will not be in my right mind. You have to make sure I don't do it!"

She promised.

HEADING SOUTH
Keeping your strategy clear but flexible

"The biggest risk is not taking any risk... In a world that is changing really quickly, the only strategy that is guaranteed to fail is not taking risks."
– Mark Zuckerberg

Long before the race began, Bill and I realised we would have to prepare ourselves better than any of our competitors to stand a realistic chance of winning. Mental attitude was vital, as explained in the following chapter, *The Final Storm*. So, too, was strategy.

In any endurance event, the race route is a decisive factor; it's even more important when you have to choose your own path from start to finish and you have to decipher the winds and currents of an entire ocean in the process. Our task was to navigate a seven-metre rowing boat across the Atlantic Ocean, from the Canary Islands to Antigua, and finish on a line only one mile wide – all without assistance or motors to keep us on track if we were blown off course.

The most direct route would obviously be as the crow flies from the San Sebastián to Antigua, a straight-line distance of about 5,000 kilometres – but these things are seldom that easy. A massive high-pressure system, the Azores High, dominates the North Atlantic Ocean, rotating in a clockwise direction and shifting slightly north or south between seasons. The direct route would ordinarily take a boat through the centre of this system, with its indifferent winds and currents.

A more fruitful plan, one followed by 99 percent of Atlantic rowers, is to follow the route most commonly used by yachts travelling from the Canaries across to the Caribbean and South America. Head south at first, with trade winds coming from the northeast, until connecting with the North Equatorial current that moves westwards at about 0.5 knots and is accompanied by the good trade easterlies to power you across the ocean. Towards the end of the race, south-easterlies then bring you back up towards Antigua.

That's the theory, at any rate, and it's a good one. The route may be a good ten percent longer than the direct line, but by optimising the winds and currents it is a lot quicker. It was the route we were planning to take.

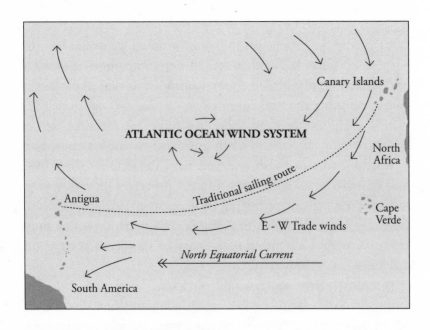

As the navigator, I had plotted a series of waypoints, which would take us on the more southerly route and which we would use as "motivators" along the way. Each time we reached one of these waypoints we would spoil ourselves with a small reward. This was a tactic I had learnt from my mind coach David Becker; breaking the race down into small bite-sized chunks would make the whole distance a lot easier for us to digest.

So we had a route strategy, and it was a good one.

Then, a week before our departure, we met up with a fellow South African, Howard Fairbank, who was undertaking a solo circumnavigation of the world in his yacht and happened to be berthed in San Sebastián while we were there. Howard is an amazing person, and we spent several days discussing our race strategy and route (and swapping the odd adventure story).

One morning, he interrupted our preparations by insisting we head to his boat for a chat. It was quite a trek to get there, but we could see he was excited and keen to talk to us without other rowers around, so we went along.

"Over the past week I have been watching the high-pressure system, trying to figure out my own route across to Panama," he explained to us, sitting at his navigation table. "And for the last few days I've noticed it moving further and further north. Now this is not supposed to be happening so early in the season, but I have spoken to my weather guys and they are all of the opinion that it's going to stay like this."

I sat there quietly digesting this news. Our carefully considered southerly strategy suddenly looked like the second-best option. But how were we to be sure?

"So what you are saying," I said, looking at the chart, "is that we could, if we wanted to, go in a straight line across the Atlantic?"

He nodded, but I was not convinced. We chatted a little more about it, and later Bill and I agreed we would watch the system closely before we made up our minds about changing route.

The high-pressure system stayed where it was for a few more days before it made another move… further north. With just two days to go before setting off on our epic race, we had a serious choice to make. After much discussion, we decided we were going to risk everything and take a chance with the straight-line route. I sat down on my bed that evening, took out the chart – already well worn with all my planning and scribbling – and started putting together the details of the new strategy. We would initially have to row south away from the Canary Islands and specifically around El Hierro, which stood directly in our way. Once we passed El Hierro we could implement our new plan, and hope the north-easterlies didn't push us too far south.

With Bill suffering severe seasickness in the first few days of the race, our initial progress was not as steady as anticipated, but we varied our shift system and finally built up a good rhythm. Once Bill had recovered, we did well to catch up with the frontrunners and soon established that *Pendovey Swift*, crewed by Ian Andrews and Joss Elliott, was leading the way.

From the information we had received from our wives, we could see that all the other boats were heading south while *Pendovey Swift* had, like us, chosen the more direct route. Before long they were also covering our every move. If we moved slightly south, they would follow. If we rowed directly east, they would do the same. They were, it seemed, strong and wily competitors.

On Day 9 of the race, the north-easterly had picked up quite considerably, and we used the opportunity to pull a bit of a tactical manoeuvre to see if we could take the coveted first position. We eased off a little and headed south, making rowing a lot easier. We knew our southerly bearing would be conveyed to *Pendovey Swift* and we waited for them to follow us. They did. That evening as the sun went down we turned west again, hardening up into the wind. It was tough going with the wind hitting us from starboard, and there would be many times during the next few days that we had to row on one side only to keep us pointed in the right direction.

The morning of Day 10 dawned with us anxious to speak to either Kim or Kate to see if our move had worked. We always spoke to our wives after the sunrise shift. This morning it was Bill's chance to go first, and before long he shouted, "Yes please!"

He looked out of the cabin and, smiling from ear to ear, conveyed the news to me: *Pendovey Swift* had continued further south and we were now in first position. Our strategy was paying off.

It's hard to describe the feeling I felt right then. It was what we had trained and prepared ourselves for and suddenly it was real. Even if we weren't able to hold on to our position, we had already proved we could lead the race.

We held our position for another two weeks, and on Christmas day we were not only leading, we were on track to break the pairs world record for crossing the Atlantic. Everything was looking really good. *Pendovey Swift* was lying in second 30 nautical miles behind us; *No Fear* was in third, 100 nautical miles behind; and *Go Commando* and *The Reason Why* were a further 150 nautical miles behind them.

We were feeling good and ready to take on the rest of the race when we received an SMS on our satellite phone; it was the Woodvale organisers wishing us a happy Christmas and informing us that they were predicting 20-25 knots of pure east wind for us. Perfect!

We decided a celebration was in order, and took a half hour off for Christmas lunch; for the first time in the race there was no-one rowing. We ate our boil-in-the-bag chicken with herb dumplings, and although it wasn't great it was a whole lot better than the freeze-dried meals we had been eating.

Then everything around us started to change. The wind stopped – a bad sign. Then it picked up hard from the north for just long enough to generate some wind swell on top of the consistent swell from the east. The wind stopped again. Then it started again, but this time it was coming from the south – the opposite direction. Two hours later it stopped again. The signs were ominous, and when it started up again we were horrified: it was the dreaded westerly headwind. On top of a 2-knot current against us. We couldn't believe it.

Throughout the night we were tossed around in all different directions as the conditions changed again and again – except for the current; that remained persistently against us. At about 2am we were very concerned by our inability to make headway into the strong current. It was time to break out the parachute anchor. This would be the first time we would use it in the race and we weren't 100 percent sure we could get it done properly in the conditions.

Deploying the parachute anchor is a rather complicated affair. With our headlamps on, we set about gathering all the parachute equipment and attaching the 100-metre rope to the bow of the boat. Once we were happy that the parachute lines weren't tangled and that the retrieval line was clear, we released it into the sea, holding thumbs it would actually work. A quickly taut bowline, also known as the main rode, seemed to indicate we'd got it right. A small victory.

HOW A PARACHUTE ANCHOR WORKS

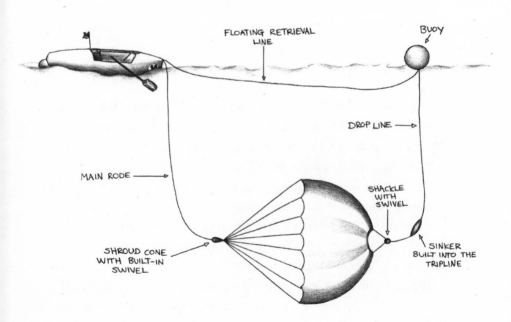

FLOATING RETRIEVAL LINE

BUOY

DROP LINE

MAIN RODE

SHACKLE WITH SWIVEL

SHROUD CONE WITH BUILT-IN SWIVEL

SINKER BUILT INTO THE TRIPLINE

Bill and I looked at each other not quite knowing what to do next. We had never shared the cabin, a tight enough fit for one person, and figured we would lie head-to-toe. We were wet, tired and very frustrated. With the boat being thrown around, sleep was impossible, and there were long hours before we saw the light of day again.

By the time the sun rose the sea was an absolute mess, with swells colliding from all different directions. How could this have all gone so wrong? Was this happening to all the boats in the fleet? As soon as I could I called Tjaart on the satellite phone. The news wasn't good.

"Pete, somehow overnight a small low-pressure system has formed and you and *Pendovey Swift* are in it," he told me. "All the other boats further south are flying and you guys are being pulled further north and away from the good winds. You need to head down south!"

In short, our straight-line strategy had just about failed us. Tjaart and I discussed the options: stick to our route in the hope that the low would dissipate, or get out of the system by heading south and pick a fight with the guys down there. If we chose option one and the low persisted, our race chances would be shot; if we headed south now, we could well give up our first place position. Neither option filled us with joy.

One of the advantages of sharing a small rowing boat with someone is that it's quite easy to organise a meeting. When Bill woke for his shift, we got together for a powwow. I told him about the call and we discussed the options. In the end we decided to head down south and pick a fight with the guys down there.

Nearly a month into the race, this was no obvious decision by any means; it was in fact a *huge* mental shift for us to make. There was the possibility we could lose touch with *Pendovey Swift* if conditions turned in their favour, and we could be overtaken by *No Fear* and *Go Commando* as we headed south. But we agreed that it was the best chance to salvage our race.

Not only did we have to head due south, but to make up the distance we were about to lose we also had to do it as fast as we could. This meant rowing together as much as possible. Initially, we shortened our rest periods to one hour while maintaining our 90-minute shifts, giving us 15 minutes together at the start/end of each shift. Then, once we were used to shorter rest periods, we dropped them further to only half an hour each. Now it was 90 minutes on, 30 minutes off, allowing us 30 minutes together at the start/end of each shift. On the one hand it was really good to have Bill's company during my shifts, and our increased speed through the water was a great psychological boost; on the other hand it was murder on our bodies. We rowed like this for three nights and three days. It was absolute hell, but our determination to win the race meant we were prepared to push ourselves. My father always told me that nothing good in life comes easily; those three days certainly didn't disprove his notion.

The race finish line, on the southern side of Antigua, lies on the latitude of 16°59' north which is just one nautical mile south of 17° north. After three days' southerly rowing we were approaching 17° north. This raised another concern for us, as the predominant winds were from the northeast, which meant that even after we turned west again, we would be pushed further south. We worried we could be pushed so far south we wouldn't be able to get back up towards the finish line, and we might even miss the island completely. Not a good idea.

Happily, once making the westerly turn and settling back into our normal rowing routine, we discovered we'd managed to cling on to our lead. Bill called Kate, who informed us that *No Fear* was lying in second spot a mere 30 nautical miles behind us, with *Go Commando* in third 100 nautical miles back.

Our risky decision had paid off, but it wasn't over yet. We would still have to work hard to maintain that lead. Over the next few days we struggled hard into a strong north-easterly wind, but we managed to maintain our heading which was a great relief. As the time passed we heard less and less about *Pendovey Swift* and eventually they dropped off the radar completely. Despite being frontrunners for much of the race, I believe their ultimate failure was the result of their inability to adapt when the conditions around them changed. They stuck to their original strategy come hell or high water, and it didn't work. They arrived in Antigua, broken, 12 days after we finished our race.

The ocean has taught me valuable lessons about planning and strategy, and our mid-race route change was a perfect example. We are living in dynamic times in a dynamic environment. It's absolutely essential to have a good strategy in place if we are ever going to achieve the visions and goals that we have for our lives; however, we must be vigilant and aware of the changes happening around us and we must be able to adapt our strategy accordingly. A clear but flexible strategy hugely improves your chances of success.

THE FINAL STORM
The importance of
a winning attitude

---

*"You were born to win, but to be a winner, you must
plan to win, prepare to win, and expect to win."*
– Zig Ziglar

From the outset, from the moment that Bill and I shook on
our decision to take part in our first Woodvale Race, we were
adamant about two things:

1. Each of us would be responsible for taking care of the other
person;
2. We intended to win the race.

Bearing in mind that I had never rowed a stroke in my life before
Bill gave me my first lesson at the Leander Club in East London
18 months before the start of the race, this second point could
have been considered a touch ambitious. (I had paddled a lot.
Paddling and rowing are not the same!) Our critics certainly
found it rather humorous and not many rated our chances, but
we believed that in a race this long the real battle would take
place in our heads. If we prepared ourselves better than any of
the other teams and if we remained mentally strong, positive
and focused, then our rowing experience and physical ability
would be very much of secondary importance.

PART I: THE LION ROARS

ATLANTIC CROSSING, 2007/8

Training session with Bill Godfrey from the Leander Rowing Club on the Buffalo River.

Inset below: Launch disaster at St Francis Bay – an inauspicious start to sea trials, but we needed to practise a self-righting roll anyway…

Two hours before the start of the 2007 Woodvale Atlantic Rowing Race in San Sebastián de la Gomera, Canary Islands, 2 December 2007. The *Gquma Challenger*, moored behind us, would be our home for the next 50 days.

The practicalities of life onboard a boat measuring 7.1m by 1.9m. Here I am chatting to Kim on the satellite phone while engaged in the tricky business of going to the loo.

Inside the cabin. Pictures of family are stuck to the roof, along with the emergency axe, to be used in the event of the boat capsizing and not righting itself.

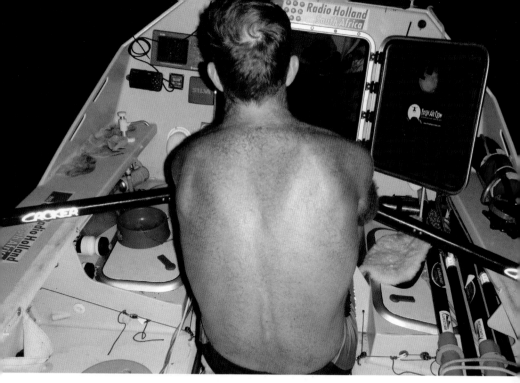

Night shift. I loved rowing after sundown. The sea is alive with phosphorescence and the stars from the middle of the Atlantic are a phenomenal sight.

My partner Bill Godfrey on the oars. Barring two occasions – a particularly bad storm and Christmas-day lunch – one of us was always rowing.

Day 23: Christmas lunch, December 2007. A grand celebration with boil-in-the-bag chicken and herb dumplings – delicious compared to our usual fare.

Nick Histon (*seated*) and the late Jon Csehi on *No Fear*. They pushed us all the way, finishing only six hours behind us.

No Fear and *Go Commando* photos courtesy of Woodvale Challenge

A mid-ocean shot of Ben Gaffney (*in the cabin*) and Orlando Rogers of *Go Commando*.

Our hands took an absolute beating.

Day 50. We are just emerging from our final storm, with about 20nm to go. Antigua is visible in the background. Having suffered no sleep over the previous four days, my eyes were deep and hollow and I was suffering hallucinations.

One of my favourite pictures. Kim, Hannah and I embrace a few moments after I stepped on to the quay in English Harbour, Antigua. It says it all: we're very emotional and very happy! Hannah hardly recognises me with a beard.

Celebrating with Bill – a lot lighter than when we started out, but victorious in the end.

With Nic "Moose" Good, who filmed our race for the television documentary *90 Minutes Closer To Antigua*, which screened on SuperSport on DSTV.

With the team that had flown from all around the world to come see us in. The tall Viking at the back is my friend Niels Andersen. Lionel and Petrea Donnelly, my uncle and aunt, are on the right of the picture.

The sign that awaited me at the top of the road on my return to my little village, Sunrise-on-Sea, on the east coast of South Africa.

Bill and I flew to London a few months after the race to attend the awards ceremony. Posing with trophies (*right*) and with Nick Histon and Jon Csehi of team *No Fear* (*below*).

Professor Tim Noakes, the renowned exercise and sports guru from the Sports Science Institute of South Africa, was involved in our preparation, and he confirmed to us that if we had any advantage at all it was that we had agreed from the beginning that we would win the race and had visualised this as a reality throughout our training.

And so, four days and about 220 nautical miles from the finish, we were delighted, but not entirely surprised, to still be leading the race. Things were going according to plan – just about. Our lead was a slim one; after 46 days' rowing across an entire ocean, John Csehi and Nick Histon in *No Fear* were only 30 nautical miles behind us and pushing us hard. Worryingly, our satellite-phone charger had packed up a few days earlier, which meant we were now unable to keep track of them. And we were in dire physical shape.

My hands were almost non-functional by this stage, and had to be coaxed into life for every shift. The first five minutes of rowing involved the most excruciating pain, which would then thankfully subside somewhat once they had warmed up. My bottom was in appalling shape. I had fashioned a new seat from foam with holes cut strategically into it, and there was some relief to be gained from plastering Sudocrem nappy rash cream into all the right places, but by the end of every shift I was in agony. There were salt sores between every finger and every toe, and in less glamorous places too. Bill was suffering similarly.

Still, this was all to be expected, and we took some comfort in knowing that the other crews would be no better off. Our spirit was good and our resolve to win was as strong as ever. We were highly motivated by the fact that our wives and families were on their way to Antigua. Our last phone call had been a euphoric exchange from a pub in the south of England where Kim and Kate and the kids were overnighting with Bill's in-laws.

But now communication was a thing of the past, and no amount of fiddling and tinkering with the phone charger would alter that. No more motivational chats with our friends and family, no more weather information, no more position updates. Bill, in particular, suffered terribly because of the sudden loss of communication with the outside world, and he had to dig deep to deal with it.

On the other hand, we were the guys with the plan to win and the "90 minutes closer to Antigua!" attitude. We quickly realised there was a positive spin: the broken satellite phone eliminated a daily distraction and allowed us to focus 100 percent on the critical finish of the race. With what looked like good weather ahead, we could focus completely on securing victory. If we'd had access to a weather report, we may have been less optimistic…

By late afternoon, a beautiful day had turned bleak and grey. Leaden clouds filled the sky and ominous bursts of lightning were visible in every direction. Without any foreknowledge, we were heading into a massive storm.

As the bad weather descended, Bill stood up on deck fed up with this turn of events and shouted, "Come on, Atlantic Ocean! We can handle anything you throw at us!" I stuck my head out the cabin looking at him in dismay and we laughed. Little did we know how we would be fighting for our lives over the next few days.

A few hours later the mother of all storms was upon us. Wind gusts blew at up to 120km/h; rain lashed us from every side; 10-metre swells topped with 6-foot white horses roared by. Visibility was so bad I couldn't read the compass two metres in front of me, and lightning was crackling all around us, much too close for comfort.

People often assume that I must be fearless or uncommonly brave to do what I do. This is not true at all. In the midst of that storm I was terrified, and that first night was hectic beyond anything I had ever experienced or even imagined. But humans can adapt to almost anything, especially if it persists for long enough – and this storm certainly did!

By morning it showed no sign of abating, and neither of us had had a moment's sleep. We were exhausted and urgently needed something positive to focus on. In this case it was the wind direction: it was blowing us towards the finish line. If it had been coming from the other direction we would have been huddled together in the cabin with the parachute anchor out, being steadily driven back the way we'd come, a terrible morale crusher.

With every hour of wind, the swell increased to enormous proportions, even 15 metres at times, making it dangerous to be on deck – so we found another positive. We figured our competitors would rather shelter in the cabin than continue rowing under such conditions, which meant we could use the storm to our advantage by toughing it out on deck and rowing through it. We would increase our comparative speed substantially and consolidate what we hoped was our existing lead.

The storm raged on relentlessly throughout the next day. For the first time in 47 days it occurred to me that we might not make it to Antigua. It was now a question of pure survival. We had gone 24 hours with no rest and very little sustenance and, although used to sleep deprivation and constant fatigue, we were beyond exhaustion. It was all we could do to focus on keeping the back of the boat into the breaking swell to reduce our chances of capsizing.

Banishing our doubts proved tricky. If our nearest rivals were on a slightly different course that kept them from the clutches of the storm, they could well ease ahead of us. *No Fear* might already have caught us... Still, this was now of secondary importance as we entertained the possibility that *Gquma*, along with Bill and I, may not make it through the storm.

Our survival demanded that we put aside uncertainty and negativity. The reality was clear; dwelling on it was pointless. Through the waves of exhaustion I reminded myself that there is no story without a struggle. Every expedition I had ever embarked upon had at some point stared failure in the face; it is the nature of these things, and it is the nature of life. Anyone can act with resolve and courage when all is going according to plan. We only truly prove ourselves when everything appears to be falling apart. This was one of those moments, and Bill and I simply had to *vasbyt* to see it through.

We reminded ourselves of the very first time we took *Gquma* out to sea, and the possibility of epic failure that presented itself then. Along with our friend and manager Dave Pattle, we had driven to St Francis Bay to collect our boat from Duncan Lethbridge, the owner of St Francis Marine who had assisted us with various alterations. The prospect of *Gquma's* maiden voyage out of the Port St Francis harbour was enormously exciting, and we had arranged for the press and National Sea Rescue Institute (NSRI) to be in attendance to record the triumphant moment for posterity. *Gquma* felt steady in the water, and after the first couple of strokes I was feeling relaxed and confident and looking forward to the triumphant moment when we would round the harbour wall and enter the open ocean.

My confidence was short-lived. Just as we cleared the entrance, a freak set of waves arrived from nowhere and rolled the boat, tossing Bill and me into the water. I somehow managed to hold on to *Gquma* and tried with every ounce of my strength to keep her off the rocks, but the waves just kept coming. In a desperate move I insinuated myself between boat and rocks to act as a buffer and minimise the inevitable damage. Disaster was imminent... but somehow we managed to attach a towrope and clear the breakers. *Gquma*, Bill and I were bruised, scratched and severely shaken. We regrouped, assessed the damage and continued with our planned outing. We had needed to practise a roll to ensure that the boat was self-righting and now we could tick that one off the list of things to do. Always looking for the positives...

It is moments such as these that define an expedition and set the scene for managing disaster when next it strikes. One of the journalists from the press boat contacted me the next day to enquire whether we were still planning to row an entire ocean after the incident. "We're having an official launch of the boat on 10 October – be there," I told him. "This boat is going to win the Woodvale Atlantic Rowing Race."

*

Given our calamitous start, it's no wonder there weren't many who fancied our chances, especially as they weren't privy to our mental preparations. I speak to audiences around the world and I frequently encounter people who have never embarked upon their journeys to achieving their purpose in life because of paralysis brought on by the fear of failure.

What will happen if things go wrong? If my plans fail? If the freak wave hits? What will people think of me?

We've all had these restricting thoughts. And you can bow to them by refusing to start your journey, in which case you will never fail – but you will also never succeed.

Whenever I am faced with these moments of fear and self-doubt, I am reminded of a speech that Theodore Roosevelt, author, explorer and president of the United States, made in 1910. His powerful words always have the effect of catapulting me out of my moment of paralysis. I have memorised the following lines and use them as a tool in these inevitable moments:

"It is not the critic who counts; not the man who points out how the strong man stumbles, or where the doer of deeds could have done them better. The credit belongs to the man who is actually in the arena, whose face is marred by dust and sweat and blood; who strives valiantly; who errs, who comes short again and again, because there is no effort without error and shortcoming; but who does actually strive to do the deeds; who knows great enthusiasms, the great devotions; who spends himself in a worthy cause; who at the best knows in the end the triumph of high achievement, and who at the worst, if he fails, at least fails while daring greatly, so that his place shall never be with those cold and timid souls who neither know victory nor defeat."

Heaven forbid that we should ever be one of those cold and timid souls!

Roosevelt's words have stood the test of time. After I recited them during a keynote address at a Hertz awards function in Johannesburg in 2011, the company CEO Joel Stransky, best known for his splendid extra-time drop kick that won the Rugby World Cup for the Springboks in 1995, was pleased to be reminded of them.

"Pete, that Roosevelt quote is brilliant!" he told me. "Just before we ran on to the field to play the All Blacks in the World Cup final, coach Kitch Christie had two things to say to us. The first was, 'Boys, I feel sorry for the All Blacks today.' And the second was the very same quote by Roosevelt."

Powerful stuff.

As night began to fall on the second day of the storm, its intensity increased. This was almost unbelievable, given the conditions we'd already endured. Getting in and out of the cabin became an immensely hazardous affair, literally a matter of life and death. When the time came for swapping positions, I would slide the seat as far forward as possible and shout above the noise of the storm to Bill in the cabin, updating him about conditions and hazards. Bill would then open the hatch and attach his feet to his lifeline leash before exiting. I would have to kneel next to the seat, holding onto it while Bill emerged as rapidly as possible, sat down and slipped into the waist harness. I would then assume Bill's position in the cabin before releasing my own lifeline leash and battening the hatch.

At about midnight on the second night, we had just performed this complex manoeuvre. I was attempting the impossible task of getting some rest when I heard a particularly massive wave smashing into the boat. Bill was washed right off the seat and would have been overboard in an instant but for the harness. He was lying next to the seat, groaning and trying his best to assume the rowing position when, in the midst of the chaos, I became aware of a flash of light. It repeated itself again and then again, at which point Bill called to me. I opened the hatch to see that the Emergency Position Indicating Radio Beacon had been dislodged and was beeping and emitting a bright strobe light. The EPIRB is a critical piece of safety equipment that may only be manually activated when your boat is sinking or there is someone aboard in need of urgent medical attention and you have exhausted all other means of communication. The fact that ours appeared to have activated automatically was not good news. Bill passed it to me and, shouting above the storm, asked me to switch it off. In the darkness and driving rain and sea spray, I was unable to work out why it had turned on or how to turn it off, so I fiddled with it a bit then pushed it under some clothes in the cabin and tried to get some rest.

When we swapped positions again, Bill mentioned that he had spotted a number of ships in the vicinity, and one in particular was getting uncomfortably close. As my eyes adjusted to the wild night conditions, I saw what he was talking about. What was happening? Were we suddenly in the middle of a busy shipping lane? It was dangerous enough to have to deal with the current conditions; adding a couple of ships to the mix could be lethal.

I could make out the lights of one ship in particular that was probably a few hundred metres away – it is difficult to judge distance at night – so I alerted Bill and asked him to get on the radio and avert a potential collision. And then through the haze of sleeplessness and chaos I began to register what had happened. The EPIRB was not malfunctioning; the enormous wave that had knocked Bill off his seat earlier had swamped us with enough pressure to trick it into believing it was submerged and activating the SOS signal. The sudden appearance of ships in our vicinity was the result of a search-and-rescue operation, with *Gquma* as its target.

We could now see the outline of what appeared to be a massive fishing vessel no more than a hundred metres away. It was so close that we were in danger of being run down. Bill managed to make contact with the ship but couldn't understand what was being said; it was all in French. Our would-be rescuers would have no way of knowing we were such a tiny vessel and would never spot us in such conditions. They might even run us over without noticing.

After many anxious minutes of calling we eventually received communication from the ship's captain. He explained in broken English that his vessel was one of numerous boats responding to a request for assistance in a search-and-rescue mission initiated by Sea Rescue in Falmouth, United Kingdom, which had received our distress signal. We had inadvertently caused pandemonium in the Atlantic by the activation of the EPIRB.

We hurriedly identified ourselves as a rowing boat taking part in an unassisted race to Antigua, confirmed that we had not intentionally activated the EPIRB and insisted that we did not wish to be rescued. There was a long silence. Then animated French discussion. It seemed the captain was trying to work out if it was possible that our story could be true. Why on earth would a rowing boat be out in the open ocean in these conditions?

I patiently continued to explain the situation and reassure the French captain that we were perfectly okay, while he kept insisting that this was a most ridiculous notion because there was no way we could be a) okay and b) sane.

The last part of the conversation went something like this.

> FRENCH CAPTAIN: "So are you sure that you are not in need of any assistance whatsoever? Over."
> ME: "Yes, thank you. We are racing to Antigua from the Canary Islands and are almost there, over."
> FRENCH CAPTAIN: "Please can you confirm what kind of vessel you are, over!"
> ME: "We are an ocean rowing boat, over."
> FRENCH CAPTAIN: "Please repeat, over."
> ME: "A rowing boat, over."

[long silence]

FRENCH CAPTAIN: "A rowing boat?! And you are sure you do not want to be rescued? Over."

ME: "Yes, thank you. We are fine and just have a few more days to go, over."

After rather a lot of haggling, I gave him Kim and Kate's telephone numbers and asked him to send a message to the race organisers and Sea Rescue to inform them we were fine and to call off the rescue operation, which was in fact putting us in new danger. On the back of some particularly disconcerted French expletives, the trawler eventually moved on, leaving us alone once again to battle the storm.

Amazingly we had covered a hundred nautical miles in outrageous conditions, but with 120 nautical miles still to go there was no rest in sight. We had not slept for a second during the storm and it was sucking every ounce of energy from our exhausted bodies. We kept at it. On day three it rained hard and continuously for 24 hours. By the evening the wind was so wild that I could not call loud enough for Bill to hear me at the change of shift. We were still getting hit side on by weird waves that would come from nowhere, completely out of sequence, and throw us off our seat.

When we couldn't read the compass we would simply row according to our instincts. This was not as problematic as it might have been, as the wind was blowing consistently from the east; we just had to follow it. Far trickier was the ever-increasing swell, also from the east, which offered extreme thrills and the danger of capsizing each time we went surfing down a monster face. When I was in the cabin I could feel immediately when the boat was about to start its surf and get on the plane, and I would brace myself for the impact at the bottom of the swell. While I was rowing, there were occasions when we would pick up so much speed that the boat would be totally submerged at the bottom and would shudder as it slowed. The fastest speed we recorded during this time was 18 knots, about 34km/h.

By the morning of 21 January 2008, after three days and three nights of mayhem, we had just about outridden the storm. Though the swell was still huge, about 10-12 metres, the wind had dropped to a manageable 35 knots and patches of blue sky were visible in the distance. Happy days. More importantly, we had only 50 nautical miles to go and, according to our calculations, would be arriving in Antigua sometime that evening. It was comforting yet weird to think that we would not be spending another full night at sea.

I was, of course, shattered. The storm had been the final test on top of seven weeks' rowing, and after three days without sleep I spent the day seeing strange white dots flashing before my eyes, as you do when you've taken a blow to the head. It was worrying enough that I had to ask Bill to keep an eye on me. Our real concern, though, was whether or not we had lost our first position. Had our marathon efforts over the last three days and nights been enough to secure victory or had our arch rivals, *No Fear*, managed to sneak past us?

Then everything happened really quickly. In my altered mental state I thought I saw a helicopter, which may have been a frigate bird, which in fact turned out to be the helicopter carrying Kim, Kate and Moose. When I raised my index finger to ask if we were first and Moose replied in kind to signal that we were, it was happy days, indeed!

The circle was complete. We had started out with a dream; a dream to row across an ocean and win the Atlantic Rowing Race. As Tim Noakes had confirmed to us so many months before, this attitude was the ace up our sleeves, a self-fulfilling prophecy ignited in our minds. We started with a winning attitude, we overcame the limitations of our minds and we won.

No Fear finished less than six hours after us. It was the

equivalent of winning a 42-kilometre marathon by 45 seconds. Rowing through the storm rather than battening the hatches had proved the difference.

GO COMMANDO
WITH JUICE BOTTLE
Efficiency and innovation –
and taking inspiration from
unlikely places

*"Without continual growth and progress,
such words as improvement, achievement
and success have no meaning."*
– Benjamin Franklin

Our flight from London to Tenerife in the Canary Islands, in November 2007, was an inspiration. Looking out over the vast blue Atlantic Ocean with its great white horses all blowing in one direction – most of which looked bigger than our rowing boat – was both thrilling and daunting. Bill and I sat quietly taking in the enormity of the task we had set ourselves.

From Tenerife we took a ferry across to race headquarters in San Sebastián on the island of La Gomera. Race rules stipulated that all the teams were to assemble in San Sebastián two weeks before the start, which would allow us sufficient time for preparations and last-minute fixes, before the official scrutineers checked our boats and equipment, including medical and food supplies.

The little port reminds me of the Karoo, with its hardy shrubs and bare mountains. The houses have a Greek island feel to them and there is a stately and ancient church in the town square. In the afternoons the shops close down for siesta before the entire village comes back to life in the evening, with children playing and riding their bikes in the square and along the waterfront while their parents gather to talk and drink wine at the pavement cafés. The whole village is injected with a sense of energy and excitement by the presence of the rowers and their supporters, and there is an enormous amount of local interest in the race.

When we arrived at race headquarters the place was abuzz. The first two rowers we met were both British Royal Marines. They introduced themselves as Ben Gaffney and Orlando Rogers of team *Go Commando*. They were huge! Both Bill and I are skinny guys. Although we had tried valiantly to bulk up before the start, I weighed in at a measly 86 kilograms and Bill was just 79 kilograms; not much of a margin to work with once you start losing weight during a 50-day endurance event. Ben and Orlando were both upwards of 100 kilos. They were also young, fit-looking fellows and we considered them to be serious competition. Their boat was new, beautiful and made from lightweight carbon, quite different to *Gquma*, a traditional wooden boat and a lot heavier.

During our first conversation with Ben and Orlando – and actually all our subsequent conversations with them – we were made to understand that they were out to win the race and break all records. They really looked the part and were being filmed for an ITV documentary. On asking them about the competition, they informed us there wasn't much and that they were only really worried about one of the girls' boats. Nice!

When our boat eventually arrived just five days before the start of the race, we settled down and worked quietly at our berth. We didn't want to let the cat out of the bag that we fancied ourselves as contenders, and we figured no-one would consider us to be serious competition.

By race day all the boats were moored along one side of the quay. It was a beautiful sight seeing all 23 rowing boats next to each other. The rowers all worked frantically, checking that we had everything we needed and all was in order, because once we pushed off the side that would be it; no assistance until we arrived in Antigua some 5,500 kilometres later.

A couple of hours before the start of the race – quite a stressful time – Ben and Orlando came over to wish us well for the crossing. They radiated confidence.

"Pete, Bill, as you know we are Royal Marines and when we get to Antigua we will probably have duties to attend to in Iraq or Afghanistan," Orlando said as we were shaking hands. "We won't have much time to hang around and will probably be gone already when you get in. No worries, though. Here is a *Go Commando* juice bottle to remember us by."

He handed us the type of juice bottle a cyclist might use. It was plain white with their GO COMMANDO logo printed on it. How generous!

Bill and I smiled and thanked them politely. We were delighted to have their memorabilia on board, but not knowing what to do with it we simply tossed it into the cabin. Little did we realise how important that bottle was going to turn out to be.

A few hours later the starter siren sounded and all the boats disappeared off towards the horizon at varying speeds. By evening we could only make out one or two boats, which had kept their navigation lights on. Ours were off. Stealth mode. The race was on.

There is always something we can do to make ourselves more efficient. Something we haven't done before.

Every single shift that we rowed on *Gquma Challenger* was different to the shift before, which meant we were constantly making adjustments. It was all about optimising our boat speed, depending on the prevailing conditions or our latest bright idea. We would regularly switch from the forward to aft position and back, depending on which was working better. We would move the 30-kilogram life raft that was lashed to the deck of the boat from the bow to the stern, or even position it next to us, depending on the sea and wind. The general rule was more weight up front when we were getting side and head winds, to keep the nose from swinging around. We would shorten or lengthen the oars to suit different conditions; the rougher the conditions, the shorter the oars. All to gain that extra fraction of a knot.

Of course, the more time we spent rowing, the better; we needed to do all we could to eliminate anything that prevented us from rowing, no matter how briefly. A couple of days into the race we identified a surprising time-waster: going for a pee. We both needed to empty our bladders about eight times a day, and urinating over the side of a rowing boat in the middle of the ocean is a more complicated affair than you might imagine. To understand it better you need to picture the scene... or at least some of it.

The act of going for a pee requires that you first pull in the oars and strap them together with the surfboard leash attached to the deck. You have to then get out of your rowing shoes (used for steering) and make your way from the seat to the side of the boat, which by this time may well be side on into the swell and pitching all over the place. You end up balancing precariously over the edge while relieving yourself, then when you are finished you have to do it all in reverse order. Even if you're the non-rower you render the boat unrowable while standing to one side of the boat doing your business.

We worked out that each time we went it was taking at least three minutes, and that two of us going 16 times every 24 hours would cost us up to 3 nautical miles a day. Now 3 nautical miles is just a chip and a putt in the greater scheme of things, but over 50 days that works out to 150 nautical miles. A substantial distance.

Enter the *Go Commando* juice bottle.

It didn't take a rocket scientist to figure out that we needed a change of pee plan, and thankfully we had a ready solution on board compliments of Ben and Orlando. The moment we worked it out, we dived into the cabin, retrieved the juice bottle and started using it immediately.

The bottle itself was the perfect receptacle for two reasons. For one, 750ml seemed to be the ideal volume. More importantly, though, it had a very wide opening which suited us to a tee. No, I'm not bragging; it allowed us not only to pee while still in our seat, but also to throw the proceeds over the side afterwards. It was a bit messy to start off with, but there was always a bit of wash over the deck so it didn't bother us too much, and after a bit of practice we tended to get it right. If you were not rowing you could just stand in the middle of the boat and do your business without disturbing the rower. Perfect.

In the end the 3 nautical miles that we saved every day thanks to the *Go Commando* boys was one of the differences between winning and losing. After our satellite phone broke ten days before the finish we had to row blind, unaware of our position in the fleet. We knew that John Csehi and Nick Histon in *No Fear* were hot on our heels, and that *Go Commando* was lying in third. Only when Kim, Kate and Moose flew out by helicopter to find us on the final morning of our race did we find out we were still the leading the pairs, and when we finally came within VHF radio signal range of Antigua we found out how close behind us *No Fear* was: a mere 25 nautical miles. Probably not more than a hundred pees.

Perhaps happily for Ben and Orlando in *Go Commando*, they were still several days from the finish and our total juice-bottle savings were less than the distance they still had to cover. Their well-intended donation hadn't cost them a place.

We had only three days in Antigua before heading home; just enough for some recovery time before the long trip back to East London via London and Johannesburg, and for us to clean and pack up the boat. When Bill and I returned to *Gquma* the morning after our arrival, we were amazed by what we saw. It looked like a battle scene, the after-effects of the four-day long final storm.

The first thing that caught our attention on the deck was the poor abused *Go Commando* juice bottle. Aware that Ben and Orlando were still four or five days out, it dawned on us that we wouldn't be there when they arrived. The irony was not lost on us, and we devised a plan. After washing out their juice bottle as best we could, we found a new lid for it and wrote on the side of it in permanent marker pen:

"Dear Ben and Orlando, well done on a great race. Sorry we could not be here to see you in! All the best, Bill and Pete"

We left the bottle with the race organisers to give to them when they arrived. I often wonder whether they ever used it afterwards, or whether it is lying on someone's mantelpiece somewhere. Either way, that juice bottle taught me an important lesson.

Peeing inefficiently could well have cost us the race. It was the perfect example of the notion that there is something we can do every day in our lives to make ourselves, our businesses and the things we do more efficient and better. Since my first Atlantic crossing, I have done my best to use this rule continuously in my life so that I don't even have to focus on it; it is simply second nature. I can't tell you what it is in your life that you can work on – but the *Go Commando* juice bottle taught me that there is always something, believe me.

A SAD POSTSCRIPT
Unfortunately, two excellent men involved in this story have subsequently died in tragic accidents, one each of the crew of *Go Commando* and *No Fear*. Both were former Royal Marines who served in Afghanistan.

Orlando Rogers was killed on 15 May 2011 in a light aircraft crash in Dorset, England. From his website, *orlandorogersfoundation.com*:

Orlando Rogers was a truly remarkable guy. He joined the Royal Marines at 18 and by his 19th birthday had become the youngest officer to pass out of training. Everyone in the Corps knew him as "The Man Mountain". He believed in living every moment as if it were his last and shared his abundant enthusiasm for adventure with all he met. In 2011, at the age of 26, his life came to a tragic end whilst fulfilling another of his ambitions – to fly in a Tiger Moth bi-plane. His memory lives on in the Orlando Rogers Foundation, a charitable fund founded by his family and friends to enable other young people to fulfil their dreams."

Jon Csehi died in a motorbike accident on 20 April 2013 in the Orkney Islands in Scotland. He was 29, and left behind a wife and young daughter. From Nick Histon, his rowing partner:

Jon Csehi was a wonderful husband, a devoted father, a perfect son and a loyal friend. I was fortunate enough to know Jon for 25 years and felt privileged to be a part of his life. The highlight of my time with Jon was in 2008 when we rowed across the Atlantic as part of the Atlantic Rowing Race. Jon showed incredible determination, resilience, strength and spirit to meet the challenge. There are very few people in life that make a genuine impact on the world: Jon Csehi did.

PART II
NOT ALONE

Two years after winning the Woodvale Atlantic Rowing Race pairs class with Bill Godfrey in 2008, I returned to the Canary Islands to row an ocean once again – but this time I would be attempting it on my own. The physical challenge of the Woodvale race is, of course, extreme, but equally daunting is the isolation. Completely unsupported, rowers must battle a terrifying sense of insignificance in the vast expanse of tempestuous blue water that lies between them and the finish. It is a sense that is magnified immeasurably when you are the only one in the boat. Though I had rowing experience now and would start the race far better prepared, it would turn out to be the toughest Atlantic Rowing Race on record, and by far the toughest physical and mental test of my life.

NYAMEZELA:
A SOLO ROW ACROSS
THE ATLANTIC

"Peter van Kets continues to push the boundaries
of his mind and body by completing adventures
that leave us speechless in wonder."
– **Professor Tim Noakes**

On Day 3 of my first row across the Atlantic, on board *Gquma Challenger*, I had a vivid realisation followed by a terrifying moment of doubt. "Oh my goodness, this is not what I expected at all," I clearly remember thinking. "What have I got myself into?"

The first crossing had been a journey into the unknown, and that in itself is an enormous X factor. But in spending 50 days in a rowing boat and completing one race, I had learnt many lessons. What could I have done differently? How might I do it better? These were the questions going through my mind early one morning in April 2008, about three months after stepping onto the pier in English Harbour and promising Kim I would never put her through something like that again. As I lay in bed reliving the *Gquma* crossing while tossing and turning and unable to get back to sleep, it dawned on me that the agony of the experience had miraculously faded away and doing the whole thing again was seeming like rather a good idea... The really clever part of my plan was that this time I should do it on my own. If things went well, I figured, I had every chance of winning the solo class.

It made perfect sense. I knew what I'd be up against. I had experienced the storms, the pressure sores, the claw grip, the tendonitis in the fingers, the blisters and raw feet, the insane isolation, the trivial yet overwhelming frustration of not being able to walk around for weeks on end, the boat that would never, not even for one second, be still for the duration of the trip... My greatest advantage in the preparation for a second race would be the simple fact that I had participated in a first race.

My experience gave me one further critical advantage: I would have a much better chance of obtaining decent sponsorship to make the whole thing financially feasible. The first crossing had pushed my personal finances to the brink. Despite the wonderful assistance we'd managed to secure, Kim and I had had to re-mortgage our house and it had been a near-run thing just getting to the start line. That scenario was not an option any more.

I approached Kim with the idea.

Understandably, she had her doubts. The memories of *Gquma* had clearly not faded as rapidly for her as they had for me. She reminded me of all the hardships I had specifically asked her to remind me of should this conversation ever arise. We discussed finances, and the difficulty of her juggling a stressful corporate job, her duties as a mother and her own personal ambitions. At the end of the conversation – and I will always honour her for this – she fixed me with a steely look and said, "Peter, you must go and do this row. I will never stop you from achieving the dreams and visions you have for your life. But you know what you are taking on this time. Don't do it lightly."

I certainly didn't. We thought long and hard on the decision, we prayed about it, and in the end we made the call that if I was able to secure a significant sponsor a year before the start of the race then it would be a go. And so I went public with my plans and the search was on once again for a sponsor – possibly the hardest part of any serious endurance event.

I was encouraged by an email from Ian Gallacher, personal sponsor of the Garmin navigation equipment that Bill and I had used on *Gquma*. His message came with a hugely generous donation to my cause: a cash deposit into my bank account, no strings attached. I was blown away. Ian had followed the first race with great enthusiasm and he was excited by the solo plan. His generosity reminded me of the wonders of the human spirit,

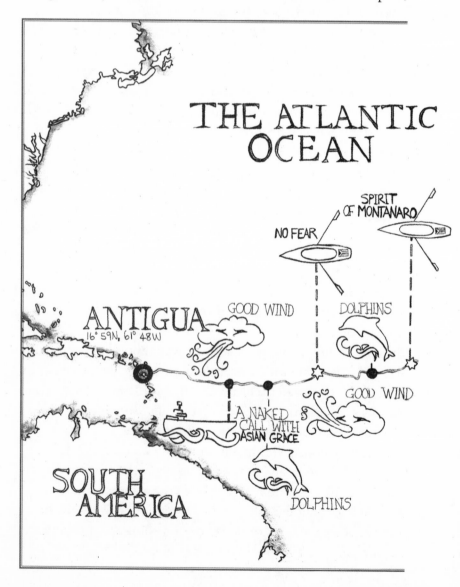

even when it is simply sharing in someone else's experience. It certainly was a sign that we were on the right track.

When it comes to major sponsorship, however, there is only one way to get it: by securing a face-to-face meeting with the decision-maker of whatever business it is you are approaching and getting him (or her) to grasp the value that could be attained. With that idea in mind, I chatted to Johnny Goldberg, a friend and

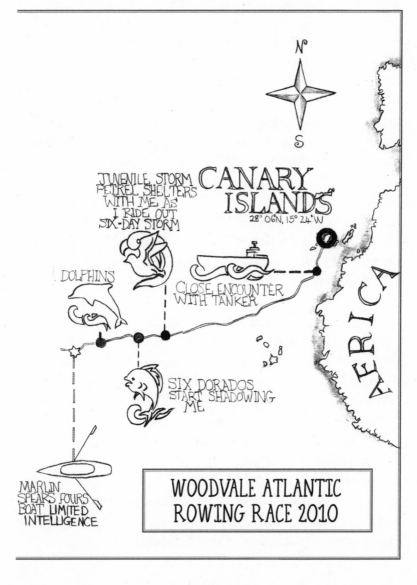

business advisor who had the clout to orchestrate such meetings. He had the perfect guy in mind: Rex Tomlinson of Liberty Life. He quickly set things up. And yet it so nearly didn't happen...

After making what I thought was a colossal blunder – realising on the morning of the meeting that I had booked my flight into Johannesburg for the following day – Johnny calmly rescued things. Not only did he reschedule the meeting, he also showed Rex the *Gquma* documentary, *90 Minutes Closer To Antigua*, in the meantime. (It helped that he was staying with Rex that night.)

By the time I made my nervous arrival at the plush Liberty offices in Braamfontein – my heart pounding, my future on the line – Johnny had, it appears, set things up on a plate for me. When Rex came to meet me in the waiting area, he introduced himself by saying, "Hey Pete, I'm Rex. It's great to meet you. You are cooked in the head, man! Come, we have lots to talk about."

He ushered me into a small meeting room and introduced me to Momin Hukamdad, the company's marketing executive.

"Momin, this is Pete van Kets," he said. "He's totally nuts but I think we're going to sponsor his next expedition."

My short presentation passed in a blur. As I finished, Rex turned to Momin and said, "This fits perfectly with the 'Own Your Life' campaign. Okay, Pete, so we like your plans and want to support you." By this stage my heart rate had gone through the roof. "Tell us, how much are we in for?"

When I told them the full amount neither Rex nor Momin flinched. It was just a matter of working out from which budget it would be drawn. Forty minutes after entering the building, I left drained but entirely elated. I called Kim immediately.

"It's done, Kim, I have my sponsor!" I told her.

"Oh my *nerves*, I don't believe it!" she replied.

I almost didn't myself. Liberty Life had agreed to sponsor my campaign to the tune of R1.5 million. It was an enormous relief, as it would allow for a far more professional approach to the race and, importantly, I would be drawing a salary, which meant the family wouldn't suffer in the long build-up.

*

Now the real preparation could begin. We live in a competitive society; to compete at the highest levels or achieve anything extraordinary, every facet of a campaign is of critical importance. Alexander Graham Bell explained it well: "Before anything else, preparation is the key to success." I needed to organise my support team, build a boat, fit it out and get training. Thousands of phone calls and emails, hours and hours of training, days and nights of boat design and building and testing, a mountain of logistics, and the never-ending worry that I'd missed a critical detail – it was all about to begin.

In gathering a team around me, I kept things as personal as possible; history and friendship is important to me and I like to go with people I know if possible.

One of my best decisions early on was to ask an old mate, Cliffy Coombe, to come on board as my manager. Previously Bill and I had shared the preparations with part-time manager Dave Pattle. Having an extra hand was key and I can't overstate how invaluable Cliffy would become, especially once we made it to the Canary Islands. He was brilliant, and together with his wife Tracey also ran my website and social-media pages.

Kim's blog: Cliffy has been Pete's friend for 15 years. Although we've always been dimly aware of Cliffy's brilliance, it was only after he and Tracey seconded me on the 100-mile Tuffer Puffer that we began to grasp the full impact of their collective enthusiasm, people skills, technical/practical/medical genius, ability to nurture grumpy athletes, etc. Cliffy cycled next to me for 80km, right through the night, singing my favourite music, telling jokes, handing me tea and sandwiches, medicating my aches and pains. They both behaved as if it was a delight to spend 24 hours at my beck and call! I'm talking about Mother Teresa, Art Garfunkel, Albert Einstein, Florence Nightingale and Marc Lottering all rolled into two pairs of cycling shorts!

Nic "Moose" Good and Tjaart van der Walt also returned to help, as documentary maker and weatherman extraordinaire, and it was great to have their familiar faces back on the scene. It was of critical importance that my physical training should prepare me for the rigours of ocean rowing while not injuring me in the process. If you can row 12 hours a day for anywhere

STRENGTH AND CONDITIONING
From Caron Williams, personal trainer:

Pete approached me for training in January 2009 to assist in preparing him for his solo race. The criteria dictated that he had to be well trained physically to endure and withstand any adversity during his long race, but at the same time he shouldn't be over-trained or peaking before the start. His training had to be designed to build up his fitness slowly over a long period of time to allow for optimal physical and mental adaption and avoid compromising his immune system at any time.

Pete's postural weaknesses had been analysed by physiotherapist Tanya Mackenzie before his first pairs race. We re-looked at these and addressed them at the start of his solo training.

Chronic Injuries:
- Left ITB syndrome
- The right ITB had been successfully operated on previously
- Trigger points in the muscles of the rhomboids and levator scapular in the right shoulder
- Right wrist ganglion and possible carpal bone subluxing

- Suffered from tendonitis in his hands and forearms after the 2007 race

Acute Injuries:
- C3 spine fracture from army
- Dislocation and repair to right shoulder

I recommended that we work on a periodised training programme over a period of 40 weeks with four separate phases.

Phase 1: Stabilisation and Adaption
Period: 8 weeks   Macro cycles: 3
Initial preparation to deal with chronic injuries and task ahead. Training focus:
- Improve posture with scapular, rotator cuff, core and hip stability exercises using stability balls and TheraBands with ascending reps or resistance
- Improve flexibility in pectorals and lumbar, thoracic and gluteal regions
- Improve proprioception by using body weight exercises and stability matts
- Strength and flexibility preparation of hands and forearms

84

between 50 days (best-case scenario) and 90 days (nightmare scenario!) without sustaining a serious injury, then half the battle is won. With this thought in mind, Caron Williams, my personal trainer at the High Performance Centre in East London, put together a multi-stage training strategy for me. Caron had helped me prepare for the *Gquma* crossing, so I had plenty of faith in her.

Phase 2: Strength-Endurance
Period: 10 weeks   Macro cycles: 3
Building up a solid strength and endurance base. Training focus:
- Enhance dominant energy system: aerobic-endurance
- Improve strength without developing large muscles, by reducing central nervous-system inhibition, using drop sets in a step-type progression
- Series of short, high-intensity, medium-volume circuit-sets with rest periods of 5-10 secs to move between exercises
- 2-3 mins recovery to move between circuit-sets and circuit-series
- Followed by a low-intensity, low-volume recovery week

Phase 3: Muscular-Endurance
Period: 12 weeks   Macro cycles: 3
The longest and hardest phase, targeting the main training goal, Pete's ability to cope with fatigue. Training focus:
- A series of long, medium-intensity, stepped, high-volume circuits with 5-10 secs to move between functional exercises using flat loading patterns
- 2-3 mins recovery between circuits-sets
- 8-10 mins recovery between circuit-series to hydrate and replenish nutrients
- Followed by a low-intensity, low-volume recovery week

Phase 4: Taper
Period: 7 weeks   Macro cycles: 2
Long taper phase to allow extensive mental and nutritional preparation for Pete to regenerate and arrive at the start line in the Canary Islands feeling strong, full of energy and invincible. Training focus:
- Series of medium-to-low-intensity, low-volume functional circuit-sets with 5-10 secs to move between exercises and 3-4 minutes recover between circuit-sets
- Systematic reduction in training duration and frequency with an increased emphasis on recovery intervals
Being away for a month (seconding Kim on a race and preparing his boat) kept Pete out of the gym in this phase. He returned for a 2-week training bout before he left. Subsequent race delays allowed an extended time for taper and also to fatten up.

In addition to the technical work I did with Caron, training became part of my lifestyle. Kim was also preparing for an endurance event, the 250-kilometre multi-day self-supported Kalahari Augrabies Extreme Marathon, and we would double up where possible. If we had to take Hannah to a birthday party, I would cycle to the venue and meet Kim and Hannah there. Kim would hand Hannah over like a baton and she would run home. If I had a meeting in town I would make sure I built in a visit to the gym. If the westerly was blowing I would leave my car in town and paddle the 30 kilometres home on my surfski.

Just as *Gquma* had been first time around, my boat would be key. I researched new fast designs and considered my options, consulting with, among others, Niels Andersen and Arno van de Merwe, two world-class engineers living on my doorstep who I also counted as friends. Unfortunately, designing and building something from scratch would be too expensive, but I made the happy discovery that a solo ocean rowing boat mould had recently been brought into the country. This gave me the opportunity to get my boat made locally rather than imported from the UK, which would save me international delivery fees, customs duties, the pound-rand exchange rate and a significant amount in the cost of carbon and Kevlar. I had opted for a carbon-Kevlar hull rather than a traditional wooden one to save weight; conveniently, these materials were considerably less expensive in South Africa at the time than in the UK.

I took my plans to Uwe Jaspersen, yet another friend and the owner of Jaz Marine in Cape Town. He is undoubtedly one of the most respected yacht builders in South Africa, especially when it comes to working with composite materials such as carbon and Kevlar, and his skills are much in demand. Despite his busy schedule, I twisted his arm and he spent three months constructing the shell of the boat for me. Uwe and his team did a superb job. The hull was light and totally bulletproof, made up like a sandwich of one layer of Kevlar, two layers of carbon then an 8-millimetre foam filling, and lastly another two layers of carbon. All of it was vacuum moulded to save on weight.

The local build also allowed me to customise many of the fittings, a huge bonus. I was hoping to improve the rowing seat and steering, and I was particularly keen on installing an external sound system with waterproof speakers. Steven du Toit from Performance Yachts, another yachting friend of mine, agreed to oversee this tricky part of the operation, and I made numerous trips between East London and Cape Town to ensure that everything was perfectly positioned for my body size.

A particularly important element of the fit was the boat's power supply, a silent lifesaver that would, most importantly, power the desalinator for my drinking water, along with the autohelm, radio, navigation system, lights, satellite phone, notebook and music system. The array of ten solar panels fixed to the stern cabin and one loose flexi-panel were sponsored by Ikhwezi Unplugged, an East London-based solar energy company. The panels were designed to generate 240 watts of power to charge two heavy 85-amp deep cycle batteries. The flexi-panel was a spare that I would lie on the deck to charge when I could. It was a setup that would, in time, prove itself brilliantly – unlike those on a number of other boats – and which could have kept me self-sufficient on the boat for many months if necessary.

A new piece of equipment, one we hadn't had on board *Gquma*, was the Automatic Identification System or AIS, which the race organisers decided to introduce from 2009 as a mandatory navigational instrument for all competitors. Developed as a means to avoid collisions between larger ships at sea that are not within range of shore-based communication systems, the AIS uses VHF transceivers to emit and receive information to and from other vessels within a certain radius. The information conveyed, some pre-programmed and the rest constantly updating from on-board GPS systems, identifies the vessel in question and provides position, course and speed data, as well as extra information such as crew size and cargo. It had recently become law that AIS be installed on any vessel longer than 100 feet and, recognising the potential of the device, the Woodvale race organisers had decided to follow suit. Good for them.

From a seated position in the boat a rower might be able to see out to 2.5 nautical miles in calm conditions with good visibility. Throw in an unfriendly sea swell, a rain squall, some mist or fog, and the regular arrival of darkness once every 24 hours, and that frequently reduces to almost nothing. More critically for a solo rower, when you're at rest in your cabin your visibility is precisely zero. My AIS equipment would now identify all sea traffic up to about 25 nautical miles away, depending on conditions. Once another vessel was located in the vicinity it would calculate the risk of a collision and, if necessary, alert me to the danger. I was very pleased to have it on board. We set it up so that it displayed on the same screen as my Garmin GPS, which I could see at all times while rowing.

I decided to call my boat *Nyamezela*, a Xhosa word meaning "to push through hard times" or "to see things through to their completion".

With shipping to San Sebastián scheduled for 19 October 2009, we had just three days to have *Nyamezela* surveyed and trialled at sea in Cape Town before putting her in a container and sending her off. After all the effort that had gone into her construction, I was particularly nervous about the sea trials. What if it wasn't perfect? What if something was completely wrong and we didn't have time to fix it? In some ways I would have preferred not to know how she felt in the water until I was in the Canaries and it was too late to worry. After numerous delays, time had simply run out.

Happily, things went well – better than *Gquma*'s disastrous first trial, at least. The boat was surveyed by the South African Maritime Safety Authority to ensure that everything was functioning correctly and that she possessed the required safety equipment; as a result, I could now register her as a ship. We also set up the Raymarine autopilot, also known as an autohelm, the automated steering system that I intended to use when resting to keep *Nyamezela* on course. I could use it while rowing as well, but I preferred to steer the boat's rudder with my feet, for two reasons: to conserve battery power and because it's much more fun that way, especially in decent-sized swells when you get the chance to ride waves.

Over the following two days Cliffy, Tjaart and I took *Nyamezela* out, first at the False Bay Yacht Club in Simonstown and then from the Oceana Powerboat Club near the V&A Waterfront. When we saw that she sat beautifully in the water we all breathed a sigh of relief. After the first few strokes, I knew that I had a winning boat and it felt as though a huge weight had been lifted off my shoulders. The second day's testing was particularly pleasing, as the conditions were slightly rougher and I had a memorable encounter with a number of local snoek fishermen that left me in high spirits. While waiting for the NSRI boat to arrive from Bakoven to monitor the trial, the men crowded around *Nyamezela* as she bobbed in the shallows, and couldn't help expressing their amazement in the wonderful Cape vernacular. They had never seen a boat like it and couldn't believe the idiocy of my plan to row across an ocean.

"*Jiissslaikit! Wat se skip is die?*"
(Gee whiz, what kind of boat is this?)

"*Dit lyk soos 'n blerrie submarine!*"
(It looks like a submarine of some kind.)

"*Wat gat tjy met die ding doen?*"
(What are you going to do with this ship?)

"*Tjy gat WAT doen?*"
(You are going to do WHAT?)

"*Neeee fok, tjy's mal! Tjy gat vrek!*"
(Gee no, you are mad. You are going to die.)

It was great speaking to them because they understood the enormity of the task I was about to embark on better than most and they couldn't stop asking me questions. I wish I could see them all again and show them footage of the race – and, more than anything, demonstrate to them that I am alive and well.

Once *Nyamezela* was packed off on her journey north to the Canaries, the frenzy of activity suddenly died down. There were still a couple of publicity interviews to navigate and a few last-minute bits and pieces to organise but the calm before the storm was upon me. I wasn't to know that it would be an extended and frustrated calm as the race was delayed repeatedly throughout December and into the new year.

After the predictably emotional last few weeks in East London – I really do dread farewells – Cliffy and I left on a jet plane and made the long trek to San Sebastián on La Gomera via Johannesburg, London and Tenerife. Our day-late arrival, following weather-related delays in Gatwick, was something of a harbinger of things to come.

Back in the familiar heat of San Sebastián, I was raring to go. Straight from the ferry terminal, we set off to inspect *Nyamezela*, who had survived her trip unscathed, along with the biltong and chocolate supplies I'd stashed inside her. It wasn't long before Cliffy and I were checked in to our self-catering accommodation and packing and wrapping my *Dankie Tannie pakkies*, the treat bags containing energy juice and snack rations to last me 90 days. (Their name was a nod to my army days.)

We would have been better off biding our time rather, as the delays were fast approaching, first a huge swathe of red tape that prevented the competitors' safety flares, without which we were not permitted to start the race, from passing through Canary Islands customs. Later an unseasonal set of enormous storms would power their way from North America across the Atlantic to deliver the worst winter in memory to Western Europe.

*

At the very least, it gave us time to meet the competition. There were seven solo rowers in the race, the most ever. My first impressions were of a focused and well-prepared collection of men, and I certainly didn't underestimate any of them, even Leo Rosette, a retired US Marshall who was attempting his first crossing at the age of 59. The other five were an Irishman, Sean McGowan, and four Englishmen, James Ketchell, Roger Haines, Dave Brooks and Charlie Pitcher. Dave was one ambitious man, intending not only to row the Atlantic but then to continue through the Caribbean Sea up the Panama Canal and across the Pacific to Australia – and he was just 24. But it was Charlie Pitcher, a yachtsman of note, who was the undoubted race favourite from the moment we saw his revolutionary boat. It was shorter than the others by at least 1.5 metres, lighter and, most significantly, had a much higher cabin positioned in the bow, not the stern. The upfront cabin was ingeniously designed to act much like a spinnaker downwind, while the aft area had a lower profile to maximise this effect.

My first impression of the boat was that, unless there was a design flaw I was missing or Charlie suffered a major disaster en route, it would be impossible to beat. It's one thing focusing on ambitious personal goals and keeping a positive attitude, but it's also important to face reality head-on. It didn't help that Charlie appeared to possess the right head for this kind of race; he had completed various multi-day self-sufficiency events, including the notorious Marathon des Sables in the Sahara.

As we came to live and work together every day, often helping and advising each other, a great bond began to develop between the competitors, and particularly between the solo rowers. On a number of occasions we enjoyed meals together and one evening we arranged a special solo rowers' dinner. In time I became particularly good mates with both Dave and Charlie, trying my best to offer the younger Dave some friendly mentoring advice, and trading competitive, but always friendly, banter with Charlie.

Dave Brooks's blog: Everyone had heard rumours about the man called PVK, the battle-hardened, ocean-rowing guru who'd won the 2007/8 race and was out for blood this year in the solo class. When Pete and Cliffy arrived, they spent the best parts of their first few days talking to the other rowers, offering advice and generally mixing in. While we were all panicking and rushing about, Pete was keeping cool and getting on with the tasks at hand. After a few conversations with him, it was interesting to see myself rationalising the preparation of the boat more efficiently and taking more time to think of the bigger picture while we were all out there.

The messages of support from home were amazing and a tremendous motivation to me long before the start of the race. One night Cliffy and I received an email from researchers on Marion Island in the South Atlantic. The attached photo showed a group of young scientists clutching hand-painted banners which declared, in untidy capitals, ROW PETE ROW!!

Of the various tasks we had to complete, one was organising my medical kit in preparation for scrutineering. We identified a few crucial items that were missing and experienced a challenging and often comic shopping spree at the local pharmacy, as Cliffy and I had to try to explain in our best Spanish – limited to *"Dos cervezas, por favor"* ("Two beers, please") – that we needed Vaseline, an eye bath and tough-cut scissors. To our great relief, all went well with the medical scrutineering. The only necessary item we appeared to be missing was a rectal thermometer. How to ask for one of those in nonexistent Spanish or sign language without being arrested for public indecency? Not easy!

As the delays dragged on, Cliffy and I did our best to educate the rowers about the magnificence of South African music and the diversity of our languages; as a result, "cultural hour" was enforced every morning in the race village. The sounds of Johnny Clegg and Savuka, Miriam Makeba, Ladysmith Black

Mambazo, Lucky Dube and many other favourites would blast from *Nyamezela*'s sound system, with Cliffy and me singing along, much to the delight of our neighbours (I think). At the end of a long, hot day, we would head to the sea for a swim and an ice-cold beer at the local pub, the Blue Marlin, the unofficial race headquarters after sunset, full of race memorabilia. A South African flag hangs on the wall with Bill and my names below it, bearing testimony to our campaign in 2007/8.

The original planned start date came and went. Cliffy had to head home to other responsibilities; his loss was made up for by the arrival of Moose and his wife, Jules, and then Kim who had decided to make the trip out to see me off. But a further delay meant she too had to head home before she could.

Kim's blog: Leaving Peter alone in La Gomera was completely horrendous – we were meant to be waving him off, not the other way around! I seem to be nowhere near as stoical as the other rowing wives whose farewells I witnessed with some surprise. "All right then, goodbye dear, I'll see you in the summer. Best of luck!" They then either shake hands or peck each other on the cheek. No stiff upper lip for me, I'm afraid. I cried the whole way to Tenerife on the ferry and the whole way to the airport until I couldn't see La Gomera any more. My heart is so sore. Still, good karma in the cabin has been achieved and that was my primary mission – there is a black bra hanging from *Nyamezela*'s mast to prove it!

The sitting around was killing me. Once the race start had been pushed out to early January, I made the decision to head back to East London for a low-profile, but spirit-lifting Christmas at home where, with the excess consumption of festive food, I managed to hit my pre-race target weight of 92 kilograms. On my return to San Sebastián, I moved in with Charlie, our original accommodation now taken by Spanish holidaymakers.

We swapped ideas and got on well enough that we even started discussing future expeditions we might try together.

Finally the news came: the departure date was set. With even more tourists around now, I had to book into *Nyamezela* for the last few nights, but I didn't mind. It was a relief to be going.

With spectators shouting encouragement from the harbour walls, we set off at noon on the 4th of January 2010. It was a beautiful day with a perfect steady northeaster blowing, just what we needed to send us on our way after weeks of terrible weather. Butterflies in my tummy turned to a pounding heart and coursing adrenaline. An ocean's worth of solitude lay before me. Could I survive it? Could I thrive in it? Could I conquer my Eighth Summit?

Looking around me as I made my way out beyond the harbour walls, it seemed that almost every boat was gunning for it like we were contesting a 500-metre sprint. One of the pairs boats, *Spirit of Montanaro*, somehow managed to row diagonally across my bow – a close call, but perhaps they were just trying to arrange a rendezvous in our future.

Once the collective mayhem had drifted off with the breeze, it didn't take too long before I found a good rhythm. The Atlantic Rowing Race is bookended by two very tricky challenges. Navigating across an ocean, subject to the mercy of its winds and currents, to cross a finish line that measures just a mile across is the second (previously discussed) one. The first is getting clear of the Canaries themselves as quickly as possible, and escaping the swirling, unpredictable currents that surround the islands. In a pairs or fours boat, this is less of a problem because there's always someone rowing. My plan was to row for six hours and then take a two-hour break before settling into my 90-minutes on/off shifts. The wind was perfect and my boat was moving well.

At sunset things started to change. The wind stopped then swung to the northwest, hitting me from the side and stirring up a messy chop. *Nyamezela* was bouncing around all over the place and I started to feel that dreaded sensation... nausea. The first sign is yawning followed by swallowing and then it's as if the glands at the back of your jaws start moving around. After Bill's horrific experience two years before, seasickness was something I dreaded. In preparation, I'd stocked up on cans of sugary stewed fruit, which is good for boosting energy levels, easier to prepare than freeze-dried chilli con carne and, terrible as it sounds, preferable to vomit. It was worth the extra weight of having some cans on board specifically for this eventuality. I cracked open some peaches, which seemed to have the right effect – for a while.

Once my marathon six-hour shift was done I couldn't wait to lie down and get rid of the nausea. I connected the autohelm device and the moment of truth was nigh: would it hold the boat steady heading in the right direction? It was not to be. There was just too much beam swell hitting the boat, so I bore off a few degrees, in a direction I didn't want to be travelling, to a point where the autohelm could just hold the boat. To add to this frustration it started pouring with rain.

The day that had begun in high spirits ended in seasickness, foul weather and an autohelm unable to handle the conditions. It was a sign of things to come.

I retired to the cabin, frustrated, and called Kim.

Kim's blog: Although goodbye number 3 was bad, this is much worse. For the first time I add worrying about Pete's safety and knowing that he is suffering physically and emotionally to my repertoire of emotions. It feels very final to know that he is now on his way.

Bizarrely, I suppose, I decided that our cat would be neutered on Pete's first day at sea so that he (Peter, not the cat) could focus on the fact that someone is having a worse day than him. The idea was for him to think something along these lines: "Gee, I am having a really bad day and am feeling seasick and sore but at least I still have my gonads, as opposed to my poor kitty cat who is now a eunuch!"

Spare a thought for poor Stitches who has been waiting for the axe to fall (so to speak) since 6 December. I am sure that both he and Peter feel some sense of relief that at least the waiting is over!

I thought the procedure would calm him down (the cat, not Peter) but woke up to the sound of smashing glass at 4am. Stitches had knocked over a glass bottle while leaping through the bathroom window. So much for calm!

I laughed out loud when I heard what Kim had done to Stitches. A little humour can go a long way to lifting the spirit (as I discuss again later in the chapter "Well, Shall We?"). I tried sleeping after the call, but it was near impossible. Day 1 was done and dusted. At least I'd escaped La Gomera's clutches and got myself into good water.

The northwester and beam swells didn't let up. I struggled to sleep or keep my food down, and three days later I was still being pushed south and east. I was genuinely concerned I might wash up on the coast of Morocco if conditions didn't change, and eventually conceded by deploying the parachute anchor. Without the second rower, I was always going to need it on *Nyamezela* more than we had on *Gquma*, but it was quite a downer this early in the race, with the sands of the Sahara beckoning to the east. To make matters worse, I'd discovered a problem with the water-resistant grease that kept the tracks of my sliding seat running smoothly: it wasn't properly water resistant and, as a result, was starting to gum up. I'd have to use squirts of olive oil every shift from here on in to keep the tracks in good nick...

It's one thing putting the para-anchor out on your own, but retrieving it is an art all in itself – a very time-consuming performance. The following morning, once the conditions had improved sufficiently, I pulled it in – a routine I would become all too familiar with, having performed it only once with Bill – and continued rowing. Later that morning I woke up to what sounded like a helicopter nearby, only to open the cabin hatch and see a large container ship passing me about a hundred meters away. It was a close call. My AIS alarm had not worked and I wasn't sure why.

I was evidently in a shipping lane, as there was more drama on the high seas later that afternoon. My (now functional) AIS alarm went off while I was back in the cabin, and I darted out to find another ship bearing down on me. This time the crew of the ship, *Finesse*, en route to the Caribbean, had in fact seen me and, curious to find out what *Nyamezela* was, brought her closer to investigate. We made contact on the VHF radio and I explained to an incredulous Russian-sounding sailor that, along with a number of co-competitors, I was in fact rowing to Antigua. After a pleasant exchange, *Finesse* continued on her way. It would be my last ship encounter for quite some time. Conditions had improved and I could finally start making some headway, out of the shipping lane and towards Antigua.

Probably one of the most valuable lessons I have learnt in my sailing experience is the importance of having a set routine. It gives structure to the day and eliminates any feeling of "What now?" helplessness. Even in the midst of mayhem, a routine provides a sense of control. Bill and I developed a very clear routine based on our 90-minutes-on, 90-minutes-off shift pattern, which we stuck to religiously. I adopted a similar routine at the start of the solo race before adapting it because of weather conditions. The rigidity of the routine is what kept me sane as I set about my daily chores: preparing food and hydration, navigating, ablutions, cleaning and so on.

Eating was a key part of the routine. I ate freeze-dried expedition food as my main meals, three times a day, with each containing approximately 800 calories. Breakfast was usually muesli or oats porridge with strawberries or raisins, while lunch and dinner could be anything from spaghetti bolognese (my least favourite, reminiscent in smell and flavour to wet, smelly socks) to Thai chicken or Mediterranean pasta and vegetables (my favourite). I usually added a big splash of olive oil to every meal for extra calories, and main meals were followed by a dessert such as custard with mixed berries or stewed apple. I supplemented my meals with my *Dankie Tannie pakkies*, which contained an assortment of treats sponsored by my local Spar in East London: chocolates, sugar-coated fruit sticks, sweets, raisins, biltong, nuts and energy drinks. Because preparing food is quite a performance, especially at night, I would further supplement my calorie intake with protein shakes during night shifts and between meals. I also had some wet rations as special treats and would occasionally enjoy olives, tinned mussels or a sachet of tuna. The gastronomic highlight of my day was 100 grams of a biltong and a small packet of cheddar biscuits that I saved to eat after the 1am shift.

I packed my food into separate compartments and each meal was a "lucky dip"; I would put my hand into the hatch and eat whatever I grabbed. (Please don't let it be spaghetti bolognese again!) I optimistically packed soy sauce, wasabi and chop sticks for the sushi that I hoped to catch. Despite my plan to consume 8,000 calories every day, I steadily lost weight at a rate of more than a kilogram a week.

Due to the amount I had to consume, I spent a lot of time preparing food, not always the easiest thing in the world in a rowing boat. On Day 15 I managed to pour boiling water on my feet while cooking in rough conditions. When cooking I would sit in the cabin with my legs on either side of the cooker, which rested on a gimbal, a swivel-type adaptor that keeps the water level while the boat rocks. In this instance, a large wave smashed into the side of the boat as I was pouring the water, sending it all over my feet. I dived into the cabin for Burn Ease from the medical kit and plastered it on. Scalded feet in the middle of the Atlantic Ocean are not a good thing. The medication worked wonders; although I immediately got blisters, I managed to stave off deep burns.

Every day I earmarked five rewards on my schedule. I had a set time for most of them, from which I would not deviate, as I am a strong believer in the power of delayed gratification and reward going hand in hand – something that tends to be forgotten in this age of instant gratification.

Two of the rewards were food-related: my biltong and cheddar biscuits snack at 1am, and my freeze-dried meals, which kept body and soul together even though they were only very occasionally palatable. The making of these meals became a steady daily ritual.

Besides those, my first reward of the day was my sat-phone call to Kim and Hannah straight after the sunrise shift. I would sit in the darkness during my hardest shift, waiting for the sun to come up and thinking about what I would say to them and the news they would share.

The next reward – subdivided in two – was my sat-phone call to Tjaart, at 6am, to discuss the weather, and my call to Cliffy, which was a little less predictable, depending on the needs of the day.

And the final reward was the most exciting part of each day, something I had planned far in advance of the race. I had put together a list of people who had inspired me in my life or who had helped me get to where I was, generally or for this particular expedition. I would think about the person for the day in question during the course of the morning, and then shortly after midday I would call them to tell them I was dedicating that day to them and that I would row 50 nautical miles in their honour while thinking of them and their families. I would spend hours planning the call and what I would say. It was a process that kept me going for many rowing shifts. Most importantly it shifted my focus away from myself and my own frustrations and suffering, helping me to avoid falling into the fatal trap of self-absorption.

The responses I got from these calls took my breath away. It was fantastic. Most people would be completely amazed to receive a call from the middle of the ocean; some would just weep. When I got back to South Africa and met up with some of those I'd spoken to, I found that the calls had often affected them as much as they did me.

Part of the daily struggle was trying to keep positive and this reward, and the others, was instrumental in doing so. My custom sound system was working out well in this regard. Another routine I had instituted was a motivational technique that broke down each shift into half-hour blocks. During the first block I rowed in silence; when I made it to the second block I could lift my spirits with some music; and when I made it to the third block I could reward myself with an audiobook. Any curious dolphins that arrived midways through a shift might find themselves entertained by a little Pink Floyd, Deep Purple or Cold Play, depending on my mood. If they arrived towards the end they could listen to, say, the tales of Robert Falcon Scott, the renowned English explorer who led two expeditions to Antarctica.

Scott and his party famously reached the South Pole on 17 January 1912, only to find that they had been preceded by Roald Amundsen's Norwegian expedition. His entire team perished on the return journey, succumbing under the worst possible conditions imaginable. Stories of hardship like this made me feel as though rowing the Atlantic was a walk in the park by comparison. I listened with awe and amazement to the detail of the hardships they endured and, taking stock of my situation, I realised I was actually in pretty good shape. Though I didn't know it, this particular book would lay the seed of inspiration for a future trip. At the time, listening to audiobooks of this genre was a way of boosting my morale while passing the time.

Those dolphins were another. They had a remarkable knack of appearing whenever I was feeling at my lowest, as if they had intentionally come to lift my spirits with their cheerfulness. They would visit in pods twenty or thirty strong, either spinner or bottlenose dolphins, curious to find out what a human was doing on a rowing boat so far out to sea, and would surround me for half an hour or more. They somehow sensed that I was struggling and seemed to outdo each other in their efforts to make me feel better.

For the first part of the race, the best close encounters with marine life occurred at night. One evening I was visited by a large unidentified swimming object that kept bumping the boat, an unnerving and yet exhilarating experience. It may have been a white-tipped oceanic shark or a good-sized turtle but I suspect it was a curious pilot whale, as I spotted many beautiful pilot whales at other times. At up to seven metres long, they are significantly larger than their dolphin cousins, but they are equally inquisitive and would swim around my boat for long periods to investigate.

One rare sighting I witnessed was a wahoo hunt around the boat. Wahoo are one of the fastest fish in the sea, and one of the few that can jump clear out of the water to take down flying fish in full flight. It was quite a thing to see in action.

Three-and-a-half weeks in, the 2010 Woodvale race was hit by the worst ocean storm I have ever experienced, the epic six-day affair mentioned in the first pages of this book. While we had been suffering difficult rowing conditions to this point, this was weather – a storm upon a storm – sent to test every drop of human spirit in our bodies. Caught up in the middle of it for six radical days, it was ultimately a profound experience for me, one in which I could plumb the depths of my soul and venture into philosophical territory beyond my previous experiences.

I survived.

It was thrilling, in a way, to come out on the other side of such an experience, but nothing would come easy for us rowers in 2010. The race was turning into the slowest in history due to the adverse conditions, specifically the lack of trade winds.

A storm is maddening and frightening and possibly life-changing. But rowing into a current that's running against you is a silent killer. By early February I was battling headwinds and difficult currents that just wouldn't let up, and had to deploy the para-anchor at the end of every shift. I adapted my strategy to row in three-hour shifts so that I wouldn't be wasting so much time setting it up and retrieving it. In the worst conditions – a headwind and a current running directly against you – the para-anchor is not even effective, as the current can actually drag you backwards quicker. At times I would manage perhaps 2 nautical miles in a 90-minute shift, after which I would be shot 3 nautical miles in the opposite direction while I rested. Although the progress of the pairs and fours is also affected in these conditions, there is always someone rowing so they just move forward slower – they don't go backwards!

After struggling with an extended spell of variable winds, mostly south-easterlies, the 14th of February finally delivered a decent northeaster – the next best thing to having my wife by my side on Valentine's Day. It was Day 41 and the opportunity to head south had at last presented itself. I intended to take full advantage of it. There was, however, a further treat in store, and what an incredible treat it turned out to be.

During the day the AIS alerted me to another vessel in the area, a few miles to the north. Tapping on the touchscreen icon to bring up its information, I was gobsmacked to discover that it was another rowing boat, *Spirit of Montanaro*, with which I'd almost collided at the start. It was rowed by two amazing young British adventurers, James Arnold and Adam Rackley. We were both headed in a southerly direction, so I decided to call them up on the VHF radio and invite them over for a chat. It was fantastic to hear some different voices – and so close! – and even more so when we plotted a course to meet up. What a moment it was when we finally managed our mid-Atlantic rendezvous. Adam recounted it in his book *Salt, Sweat, Tears*, published in 2014.

As *Nyamezela* approaches, Jimmy ducks into the cabin and comes back out with the video camera. For modesty's sake he has also put on some shorts.

The camera's running.

"Hey, Adam, do you want to explain what's going on?"

"We're just popping in to see Peter van Kets. We're in the middle of the Atlantic Ocean and he's just arrived.

"We're slap bang in the middle of the Atlantic..." Jimmy continues.

"...after rowing fifteen hundred miles..."

"...and there he is."

Jimmy turns the camera to *Nyamezela,* which is now twenty metres off our port side.

A South African flag flies proudly from the stern and Pete is wearing his team T-shirt, with "Own Your Life" written across the chest. Even from this distance, we can see that he has lost a lot of weight, he looks shrunken, hollowed-out. He's really suffering. I remember meeting him in our first week on La Gomera and finding him friendly but somehow distant, his mind already steeling itself for the ocean. Now I understand.

"How you doing, man?" I ask.

"How does it feel to see another face?" asks Jimmy.

He cracks a familiar smile.

"So weird, man! It feels so good. How you doing?"

"A few blisters but in good condition," replies Jimmy. "How have you found this crossing compared to the last one?"

"Ha! A lot slower. I think I enjoyed the pairs crossing more."

From the way *Nyamezela* moves in the swell we can see that it is extremely light and as soon as Pete stops rowing, the wind blows him away from us. I paddle briefly to keep us within talking distance. Jimmy puts down the video camera and explains about his sores, which are getting worse and worse. Perhaps Pete has some advice?

"Here, let me give you some stuff... it's miracle cream."

Pete ducks into his cabin and pulls out a clear plastic tub.

"What's in it?"

"It's eucalyptus and olive oil and some other stuff. Natural oils. I told these guys what I was doing and they made it up for me. It's miracle cream." [...]

Jim and I want to do something for him. We suggest swapping some rations, but he has the same Expedition Foods freeze-dried meals as we do. We offer him some biltong, but he has plenty of that too, so Jim digs around in the treats bag and finds our last fruit bar. The sea is too rough for us to pull alongside, so I dive in and swim over to his boat. While I'm clinging on to *Nyamezela's* grab line we shake hands.

After half an hour we say farewell to Pete and go our separate ways. The wind catches *Nyamezela* and we soon lose sight of her in the swell. Jimmy and I and our little boat are alone again on the ocean. But the meeting leaves us in high spirits and over the following days laughter and thoughtful gestures come more easily."

Like Adam and James I had also been buoyed by our meeting; what a wonderful distraction it had been. I am not sure if this was the very first ever meeting between two rowing boats in the middle of the Atlantic Ocean, but it was certainly one of the first. In previous years boats could have passed a mile from one another and not been any the wiser. The AIS was proving fabulous for networking. To top it off, I later found out that my miracle cream, referred to as "Pete's Bum Balm" by its makers, Casa Castile, had helped clear up James' chaff. That must surely rate as one of the strangest pharmacy deliveries ever made...

Amazingly, just two weeks later I had a very similar encounter. During one of my early morning sessions, I noticed another vessel in the vicinity on my AIS, and when I brought up its information I could hardly believe my eyes. It was once again another rowing boat. But not just any other rowing boat; it was *No Fear*, the exact same boat Bill and I had battled against two years before. This time around, though, there were two different oarsmen on board, Richard Hoyland and Steven Coe.

I tried to make contact with *No Fear* using the VHF radio but they were evidently out of range, and there followed three tantalising days during which I could track its progress 15 nautical miles or so beyond the northeast horizon but could not communicate with it, or could communicate only partially.

Though I would obviously welcome a possible rendezvous, there was no way I was going to alter course to get within working radio range; giving up even a single mile was unthinkable. As the days passed and Richard and Steven slowly gained on me, we exchanged some radio-speak snatches of info that proved almost as frustrating as they were cheering. Human contact after so much solitude would be a huge morale booster, but modern technology was proving fallible as the two boats played cat and mouse in unhelpful weather conditions. I subsequently discovered that the aerial on *No Fear* was faulty.

Then, early one morning, when the gap had closed quite significantly, I managed to make contact. As Richard and Steve put it in a subsequent email to Kim, "This time it was the most amazing call we would never have predicted to have received whilst rowing the Atlantic. It was Pete. We were literally only hundreds of metres apart. He asked if we would like to join him for a cup of tea… I said quite matter-of-factly, 'How very English! We would love to.'"

We did indeed meet up that day, under perfectly still conditions, though we didn't bother with the tea. Richard swam over to *Nyamezela*, and the three of us shared a good 45-minute *bosberaad* – or whatever the mid-Atlantic version might be called.

"It made our day and probably the voyage that we met up this way and under the trying and testing weeks we had been enduring," wrote Richard and Steve. "It lifted our spirits enormously to share a few moments with Pete."

Their thoughts were reciprocated exactly, and particularly because Richard and Steven were both such superb chaps. As it had been with Adam and James, it was disappointing to say goodbye and have to return to the routine and the slog. When we left each other they continued tracking directly west and I headed a bit further south. This would eventually pay huge dividends for me when I found the right wind and managed to finish ahead of them – and it meant I could line up a few cold beers for them in Antigua, as I'd promised. Ultimately *No*

Fear would be the boat that came in just behind me in both my Atlantic crossings, quite a coincidence.

By now I was past the 1,000-miles-to-go mark. As Bill explained in a race update on the blog, "the drop from four digits to three is a massive psychological boost". He was spot-on. And his words offered great encouragement. "The feeling of 'this is never going to end' becomes less. As far as I'm concerned, it's just that little push for the finish (a chip and a putt, as Pete would put it) and our boy will be sucking down an icy-cold beer and sinking his teeth into a juicy steak once again… For the first time in the race, the accomplishment of rowing across an ocean and getting to the other side is tangible."

I was getting there. I had become used to my new existence and routines in a race that differed from my first crossing in so many ways. At one point it occurred to me that the patterns of my day were more like that of an animal than a person. I would come out of my hole, sniff the air and test the conditions, row, sweat, eat, drink and return to my hole – and so it went hour after hour, day after day.

I somehow got my head around the bizarre currents, unfavourable winds and disappointingly slow progress. I consciously tried to be grateful for the experience I was undertaking, I took consolation from interesting encounters with nature (and now occasionally man), and I was buoyed by occasional good days. I kept at it.

With 450 nautical miles to go, the news that Kim had booked flights to Antigua for her, Hannah and Moose was a godsend. The end was tangible.

Of course it brought with it its own specific concern: making it to the finish line at Shirley Point outside English Harbour in Antigua. The winds on this crossing had been so difficult to predict, I was paranoid we'd get it wrong and I'd end up shooting right past. It would be failure at the last: something I'd worried about the whole way across the Atlantic.

At this point I was sitting furthest south out of the entire fleet, banking on predicted southeasterly winds to take me home in the final stretch. But northeasters are in fact more prevalent in these latitudes in March, and I was incredibly anxious they would revert to the norm. In the final week I drove Tjaart to distraction, obsessively checking in with him for updates and sending a barrage of questions each time I did. Tjaart remained calm and meticulous and never showed any outward signs of annoyance or stress – the perfect weatherman to the very end.

Cliffy's blog: Well, it's nearly over! For the last 70 plus days Pete has had the entire Atlantic as his playground but the next few days and hours are crucial. Pete now has to thread *Nyamezela* through the eye of a needle by navigating between two markers one mile apart. If the currents are pulling in a particular direction Pete could miss the finish. It's happened in the past – rowers have missed the finish and have had to be towed back because they can't row against the strong current.

Luckily, things worked out perfectly, and exactly as planned for the very first time in the race. With 300 nautical miles to go, I pointed *Nyamezela* straight at the finish line, and things were starting to look great. My boat speed increased, the water felt like silk, I had favourable current for the first time in weeks and I was a happy man. The autohelm was working like a dream and I loved the feeling of earning free miles when I was taking a break. I was averaging 3.5 knots on oars and 1.5 knots when off. If only it had all been this pleasant!

I picked up so much speed in the last week that I had to constantly revise my estimated arrival time. By the time Kim and Hannah arrived in Antigua I was flying at 4 knots, far ahead of schedule. The race support yacht, *Aurora*, was due to pay me a visit that afternoon, with Kim and Moose hoping to follow suit by helicopter afterwards, and the conditions were getting better and better. It was a beautiful day, with birds diving, schools of small tuna leaping and the water sparkling; I was filled with anticipation!

About an hour before sunset, having met up with *Aurora*, I spotted a dot appearing from the direction of Antigua. Slowly it grew into the shape of a helicopter and then there it was above me, with my wife and cameraman as well as Shelly Chadburn-Barron, a South African photographer living in Antigua, looking down and waving in delight. They were circling right above me, low enough to make eye contact, and a huge lump came into my throat as the enormity of my adventure washed over me. With two of the doors removed for better filming, I could clearly see everyone in the helicopter – and specifically I could see that Kim was in tears. I was overwhelmed with emotion and soon followed suit. Kim and I made our "I love you" sign to each other and there were thumbs up all round.

I waved my South African flag, blew my vuvuzela, punched the air in triumph and cried almost non-stop for the half hour they flew over me. It's hard to describe that time – it was surreal, like I was in a wonderful dream, and certainly one of the greatest moments of my life. And when they were gone I slowly followed them towards Antigua – alone again, but not for long.

This time around I planned to arrive in daylight, and to do so I actually had to slow down in the last few hours. I got off the oars and allowed the boat to drift for a while as I contemplated my journey and made my final navigational calculations. At about midnight I was able to make out the lights of Antigua in the distance. What a sight! After 75 days at sea, and weeks of loneliness, frustration, pain and deprivation – and times when I thought I would never make it in one piece – there it was: Antigua! I offered up a prayer of gratitude. What a beautiful night it was: a light 10-knot southeaster was blowing, the current was still in my favour, and my face was aching from smiling. To top if off, I had set my personal record for the crossing: 67 nautical miles in a day.

Perversely, after going as fast as I could for 75 days, as dawn broke I desperately wanted to slow things down and relish the moment. Antigua was beautiful beyond description in the soft light of the early morning sun. I wanted to take it all in and make the moment last. This was my summit moment, like sitting on top of Mount Everest – the moment I had been dreaming of for months that I now didn't want to end.

The race finish line is one nautical mile due south of Shirley Lighthouse and about 1.5 nautical miles away from the dock at English Harbour. An Antigua and Barbuda Search and Rescue rubber duck, which had been sent out to escort *Nyamezela* in, sounded the hooter as she crossed the finish line, and I stood up on my boat, looked up at the heavens and thanked God with all my heart for getting me there safely. I then punched the air in joy, let out an almighty bellow of triumph and relief and blew my vuvuzela for all I was worth!

Kim: Having Peter in the middle of the Atlantic for 76 days was characterised more by downs than ups...but day 75 and 76 almost made up for the downs. Nothing can begin to describe the feeling of finding the tiny dot that was Nyamezela – it is really only at that moment, with 360° of ocean hemming us in, that one can begin to understand the massive extent of the loneliness and isolation that he has faced for so long. We circled so low over Peter that we were able to make eye contact – we were all shouting and gesticulating and beaming and weeping into the chaos and noise and it was the most exhilarating and moving moment imaginable. We couldn't bear to leave him and must have circled him for about 25 minutes before the fading light forced us to head for home. How awesome to know that he was okay – painfully thin and marvellously furry but strong and determined and very close to home. Sleep was impossible on Peter's last night at sea, and when he called at 3am to say he would be in by 9am we were all awake and raring to go... Then he was stepping off the boat into our arms in a blur of noise and flares and excitement and champagne bubbles and the joy and relief of knowing he was safe is indescribable. And now it feels as if he has never been gone and I have to keep looking at his beard to remind myself of the enormity of what he has achieved. Hannah can't keep her hands off it and wakes up in the night to stroke it and check that he is still here. Every day he looks a little less haggard and sunken-eyed and slightly less skinny and exhausted – the ability of the human body to restore itself is amazing. And Hannah and I are reluctant to let him out of our sight and are relishing every moment of being a family again.

My arrival on land felt like an extension of my dream – into the arms of my family, with of course a promise to Kim that I would never attempt another ocean crossing like this... And then the dream had me being led to a perfectly set table under an awning with a full English breakfast waiting for me – the first meal I didn't have to drink out of a bag in 76 days. What bliss.

I had lost 15 kilograms in two-and-a-half months, and my programme to regain the lost weight started immediately and in earnest. The English breakfast was followed soon after by a burger and chips for lunch, and steak, egg and chips and rum-and-raisin ice cream for dinner... You really cannot understand how sweet it all tasted...

I went to sleep on my first night on land clean and dry in crisp white sheets with my belly straining at the seams and my wife and daughter in my arms. I felt as if I had died and gone to heaven.

I spent two weeks in Antigua recovering and attempting to rid the island of piña coladas and pudding. The timing was perfect as we were able to watch many of the other rowers come in to English Harbour. Every time I saw a boat arrive and watched the reunions on the dock I was overwhelmed with emotion.

Unsurprisingly, Charlie Pitcher took the solo line honours, in an incredible 52 days. I was proud of my second place under trying conditions, and the brilliant young Dave Brooks, who I had chatted to regularly during the course of the race, was third, two days behind me. (Unfortunately he wouldn't go on to complete his Pacific crossing as planned; the Atlantic proved too hectic. I am sure the future has many more expeditions in store for him, though.) Roger Haines followed Dave in 92 days, another impressive feat, given that he completed his race in a pairs boat. Leo Rossette spent 101 days at sea, and unfortunately missed the finish line, being blown on to Les Saintes on the island of Guadeloupe to the south of Antigua. James Ketchell made it to Antigua nine days after that, and last on the water was Sean McGowan, who spent a mind-bending 118 days rowing the Atlantic. Both James and Sean had to be resupplied en route, an indicator of just how unfavourable conditions had been.

And then I was boarding a Virgin Atlantic Boeing 747 for a journey back across the Atlantic that would be 150 times shorter than my previous one. As we took off over the great blue wilderness of the ocean, I looked out of the window and was filled with a mixture of emotions. I was so thankful I had made it, but there was also a sense of loss. One of the greatest expeditions I could partake in was behind me; it was over. It had been epic. Some days it was as if the ocean's cruel purpose was solely to break you, as it chipped away at your resolve bit by bit, wearing you down to a primitive state, taking you beyond any limits you thought you had, and then some.

I had survived. I had conquered the Eighth Summit.

SIMON
Surviving the storms

"If you're going through hell, keep going."
– **Winston Churchill**

To adapt a well-known mariner's quote, ocean rowing boats are always safe in harbour, but that's not what ocean rowing boats are for. You have to take them out beyond the breakers to validate their existence. Accordingly, one of life's guarantees is that if you expose yourself to the open ocean – that is, if you take any risks or set yourself ambitious goals – you will encounter storms and hard times. It's easy to push forward when all is going well and to plan; no great character is required when your path is free from obstacles and difficulties. It's in the storms that the extent of your commitment and passion and your true ability to achieve great things is determined.

I am all too aware that both my generation and those that have followed are, on the whole, lacking in a certain toughness that characterised my parents' generation. When we are tired, we stop; when we are bored, we immediately change plans; when we feel the first twinge of pain, we medicate. Endurance of any discomfort is not something to aspire to. Of course I'd say that, being an endurance adventurer, but it seems undeniable that when people of today are faced by adversity, they typically take the path of least resistance or simply give up. The idea of pushing through hard times seems to have lost any of the appeal (or necessity) it may once have had.

PART II: NOT ALONE

ATLANTIC CROSSING, 2010

Construction of *Nyamezela* at Jazz Marine in Cape Town. I had only three days for sea trials before getting her shipped to San Sebastián on 19 October 2009.

Preparing myself for scrutineering, the thorough inspection of my race supplies by officials. I would eventually have 300kg of equipment on board.

Marion Island photograph courtesy of Riaan Loubser

After the initial start delay, Kim flew in to San Sebastián to visit. The support from family, friends and strangers was amazing, and included (*inset*) a wonderful message from scientists on Marion Island in the southern Indian Ocean.

The solo rowers: Roger Haines, James Ketchell, Charlie Pitchell, David Brooks, me, Sean McGowan, Leo Rossette (aged 59!). *Inset:* With Cliffy, manager and star.

Admiring my ablutions bucket "Julius My Emmer", named for Julius Malema.
Perhaps you have to have a (terrible) sense of humour to row across an ocean...

Early-morning focus. I rowed for
90 minutes on and 90 minutes off
for 76 days, and would eventually
lose 15kg in the process.

The calm appearances are misleading: the current was strong, and directly against me at this point – often pushing me backwards when I stopped rowing.

Inset: Day 55. A mid-Atlantic encounter with Richard Hoyland and Steven Coe on *No Fear.*

Day 43. My first spirit-lifting ocean rendezvous, this time with James Arnold and Adam Rackley on *Spirit of Montanaro.* Yes, Adam is rowing naked.

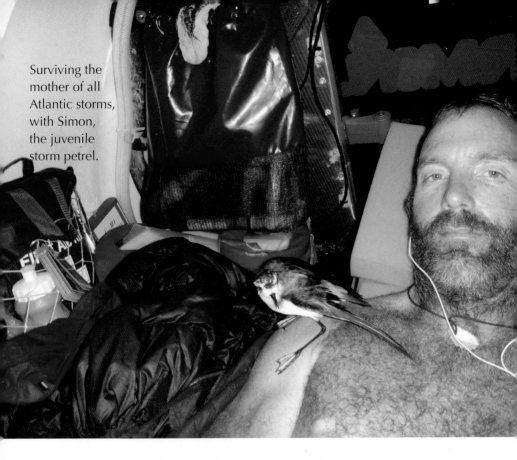

Surviving the mother of all Atlantic storms, with Simon, the juvenile storm petrel.

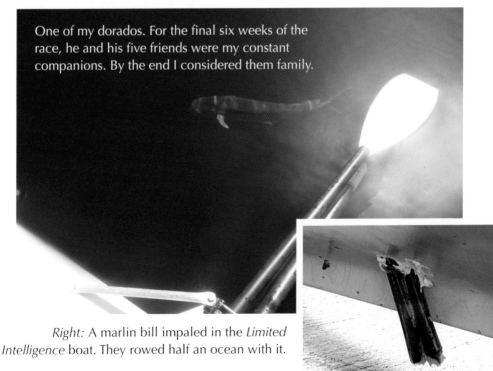

One of my dorados. For the final six weeks of the race, he and his five friends were my constant companions. By the end I considered them family.

Right: A marlin bill impaled in the *Limited Intelligence* boat. They rowed half an ocean with it.

Aerial shot of *Nyamezela* taken the day before I finished. It felt surreal to see Kim, Moose and Shelly in the helicopter after 75 days alone at sea. *(Photograph: Shelly Chadburn-Barron)*

Flying fish attracted predatory birds and fish, including my dorados. They provided plenty of entertainment, sometimes flying into the boat and once knocking me off my seat.

This is what I looked at while rowing – the mantras written on my cabin helped me through the darker days.

More encounters. The grain ship *Asian Grace* (*middle*) changed her course to witness the curiosity of a rowing boat in the mid-Atlantic. *Aragorn of Dublin* (*bottom*) sails by, having left me a much-appreciated hamper of beer and scones.

Above: The ecstasy of the end – just moments after crossing the finish line near English Harbour, with Shirley Heights behind me. *Below:* A view of English Harbour lagoon from our chalet. After the race I spent two weeks with Kim and Hannah in Antigua, valiantly trying to rid the island of piña colada and pudding.

I have learnt one very valuable lesson from my sailing and rowing experiences: the storm will end. It may rage on unabated for days, but every storm I have ever been in has come to an end eventually. To get me through the dark days of my solo crossing, I had a mantra written on my cabin: THIS WILL END! And indeed it did.

Ironically, though avoiding confrontation and quitting when the going gets tough have become more and more acceptable in the modern world, people still judge us by how we respond in times of crisis. How we perform when things are going well doesn't matter nearly as much; it is our actions during the tougher moments – or days or weeks or months – that reveal our true character.

Will we emerge from the storm strong and intact and ahead of the pack? The attitude we take into the storm, and what we choose to do once in it, will be the deciding factor.

Before the first race across the Atlantic on *Gquma Challenger*, Bill and I realised that our reaction to stormy weather would play a huge part in our success or failure. We realised that most rowers battened down the hatches and played it safe when conditions were wild. In response, we decided to take advantage of these times. Not only would we continue through hostile conditions, we would in fact shorten our rest periods from 90 minutes to 60 or even 30 minutes. We would still row for 90 minutes a shift but the shortened rest periods meant we would row in tandem at the beginning and end of each shift.

The strategy worked. While other rowers huddled in their cabins with their boats on parachute anchor or using their drogue chutes, we forged ahead even faster than usual. Unsurprisingly, there was a price attached. It took a great deal of resolve and energy to get out on the rowing seat in a raging storm in the middle of the night when our hands and bottoms were in tatters and all we wanted was to curl up in the cabin in the foetal position. We were encouraged to push through because we knew the storm would end and that when it did we would be way ahead of the pack. The lead we were gaining trumped the suffering we had to endure.

Having experienced Atlantic storms on *Gquma* with Bill and on various yachts, I knew what to expect. What I didn't know was what it would feel like to face a storm alone. During the two years of preparation for the solo row, I often wondered what it would be like to endure a mid-ocean tempest with no-one around to share the psychological burden or to help with complicated physical tasks such as putting out or pulling in the drogue or parachute anchors. Just over three weeks into the race, the time to stop wondering arrived.

For several days Tjaart had warned me of the impending storm, with the possibility of a second one to follow hot on its heels. I knew it would be coming from the south and heading north, in the same direction the current had (rather bizarrely) been moving for a while – a direction I did not want to take. My intention, then, was to head as far south as possible before the bad weather arrived to pre-emptively make up the distance I would lose when I was forced northwards.

Tjaart had established that the bad weather would arrive on 27 January. When that day broke it was so still and beautiful it was hard to believe that anything sinister was brewing. The proverbial calm before the storm.

Much like the feeling of being forced to wait nervously for a caning outside the headmaster's office, anticipating the storm was probably more terrifying than the storm itself. It helped to take my mind off things when I received my first sat-phone call from Dave Brookes that afternoon. He was about 150 nautical miles behind me in third place. It was fantastic to hear his voice, and he told me he had used the day of calm to clean his boat's hull, an experience he'd found truly terrifying and one that left me weeping with laughter.

Dave Brooks's blog: The time had come for me to brave the ink and give the old girl's hull a scrub, something I had been rather nervous about doing, as you never know what might be lurking in the gloom with no-one watching out for me on deck. Gingerly, I lowered my torso in, dangling over the side of the boat with my legs hitched around the hand rail, and scrubbed the sides of the hull, removing with my window scraper the small molluscs that were dangling off like bogies. Once I had done this on both sides, and was content that no 'orrible beasties lay in waiting, I went in for a dip, and to finish off the bottom, bow and stern. I made sure to tie myself on with the 25m throw-line and I even strapped my knife onto my upper arm just in case. Like that would make any difference whatsoever!

I remember, vividly, the conversation I had with Peter van Kets back in La Gomera about my concerns about mako, great white, white tip and hammerhead sharks. His remark was, and I quote verbatim, "Don't worry about it, bru... There's nothing to worry about, and besides, if a shark really wanted to eat you you wouldn't even know about it. You wouldn't see him circling like in the films. He'd just come at you from below!" Now I know that is supposed to be some kind of South African form of reassurance, but, WHAT THE HELL?! I did ring him straight after to tell him what I did, and he was very pleased for me, but mentioned that he'd been in loads of times before and quite enjoyed it! Ho hum!"

By sunset the wind from the south had set in and the storm was well and truly on its way. I tried to row for as long as possible into the wind. I knew that every hour of forward progress I could manage would count in my favour and clock up at least another nautical mile of good ground. By now the sea was starting to pick up and small waves were crashing over the port bow. Dave, suffering even worse, described the frustration of such conditions:

I wanted to be certain that being on the para-anchor was the only option available to me, so I hauled it in and then had a row for an hour into the weather. 1 hour's progress saw me move 500ft in the right direction, then I stopped to have a quick drink and scratch my back and I drifted back 800 yards! A complete farce!

The storm had only just begun at this point; I was yet to experience it at its full intensity. By 4am the following morning, however, I had, like Dave, given up trying to make any progress into the howling wind and deployed the para-anchor. I was heading north fast.

What a nightmare. The direction I needed to travel was southwest, certainly not north or east, yet I was powerless against the combined wind and current. Unable to row, my time at sea would be greatly increased and it looked like any chance of achieving my original targets was about to be gone with the wind – and the storm proper hadn't even reached me yet. The estimate was that it would last five days.

Then it was upon me.

Cliffy's blog: The storm that Pete is experiencing is not the type of storm that we might look forward to – no cosy couch, burning fire, good book, blankie and hot chocolate. No, nothing like that. It's the tin-can analogy. Imagine being alone in a can inside a washing machine. The water is warm, and the heat is getting turned up. It's dark in there, in that washing machine. What to do? Watch a movie? Read? Well, the fact is that all you want to do is get out that tin can and row. Instead you're stuck inside. It's getting hotter and stickier and the minutes just drag by. You can't cook because your cooker is outside and you will get burned or lose it over the side should the boat roll too much. The treats in the *Dankie Tannie pakkies* that you were enjoying are now tasting sickeningly sweet.

The sat-phone is your lifeline. It connects you to the outside world. It's a handheld entertainment tool as incoming SMSes lift your spirits. Phone calls lift you... and then drop you. The battery power sustains... and then drops as the sun's power weakens behind the grey clouds. Waves lift and drop you. Your whole world is hanging... tumbling... getting lifted up and dropped. Your emotions are fragile. All you want to do is row because you're a competitor, and although it's painful to do, anything is better than this damp, moist, view-less cabin – and anything is better than getting blown backwards over miles that were hard-earned with your sweat.

For the next five days I was an inmate of my coffin-sized cabin, constantly thrown about amid an unceasing ocean roar that was magnified by the carbon skin of the boat and made sleep virtually impossible. Most frustratingly, there was very little I could do to keep myself occupied other than some electrical maintenance, reading, watching a few movies while I still had battery, and chafing at the bit.

On the first night of the storm the sat-phone ran out of battery and I was unable to charge anything until the sun re-emerged. The absence of outside communication left me feeling very isolated, as I knew it would, and I was delighted when the sun miraculously showed itself briefly. I quickly charged my depleted batteries and I managed to make a call to Kim, my lifeline.

Kim's blog: Two massive waves broke over Peter's boat while I was talking to him and it seems that squalls and 35kt winds are predicted for the rest of today. Pete is very uncomfortable at the moment from being constantly flung around his cabin, his lower back is painful and he is finding it very unpleasant to keep his hatches closed – his choices are unbearably hot and stuffy or soaking wet! Nevertheless he is in good spirits and is delighted to be halfway through the storm already (hopefully!). He is also relieved not to be sharing his already cramped cabin with another rower, as all the pairs and fours are having to do.

Late on the third day of the storm something incredible happened.

The wind was howling outside and the para-anchor was straining against the bow of the boat. *Nyamezela* was making worrying groaning sounds, as though the anchor was trying to pull the boat apart, and I felt I needed to venture outside to see if everything was okay. I opened my hatch carefully, timing the waves to ensure I didn't flood the cabin, and stumbled the length of the boat to the bow to check the connection and the para-anchor's line. I was relieved to find that, despite the noises, everything looked good.

As I lurched back to the cabin, I glanced momentarily into my footwell. Why I did this, I couldn't say – and now that I had I could hardly believe my eyes because there, floundering around in a puddle of water, was what appeared to be a juvenile storm petrel. The poor little creature looked absolutely exhausted, and when I reached down to pick it up it made no attempt to fly off. It was finished. Not knowing what else to do, I placed it in the cabin and quickly followed, closing the hatch behind me before the next wave hit.

Though the smallest of all sea birds, storm petrels are strictly pelagic, spending months at sea and only visiting land to breed. That the storm had forced this little guy to crash land on my boat was a further indicator of its severity; even the ocean locals weren't handling it.

My new visitor was understandably anxious; he fled into the furthest corner of the cabin and disappeared under a bundle of clothes. He soon stopped moving and I assumed he had fallen into an exhausted sleep. It was reassuring to have him in the cabin and eventually, despite the noise and movement, I managed to follow his lead.

When I awoke a transformation had taken place. The little petrel was confidently strutting around the cabin as if he owned the place and I was there on sufferance. He appeared totally unconcerned by my presence. I decided to name him Simon after Paul Simon and Ladysmith Black Mabazo who sang the song *Homeless*. He was, after all, homeless and in need of a safe place to take refuge.

Simon and I cohabitated happily side by side for the next three days. He seemed very content and his presence took my mind off other things. I was concerned that he wasn't eating or drinking anything. Sea birds like Simon are adapted to drink seawater without suffering any ill effects. They have a gland behind their eyes that sieves excess salt from their blood and eliminates it via tiny tubes that drain into the bird's nostril, creating the appearance of a runny nose. I kept offering Simon what I thought were irresistible seawater tipples, but he wasn't keen on sampling any of them. Then, as he became increasingly confident and happy to stand or sit on various bits of my anatomy, I worried that I would crush him when I was flung around the cabin by a wave. This further interrupted my troubled sleeping patterns, as I would constantly wake to check he was still in one piece. But of course I was ecstatic to have a companion with me while I was confined to the cabin for such an extended stay. Simon's presence was a huge morale booster and we became, for our short time together, bosom buddies – literally, he sat on my chest a lot!

The weather forecast showed that we had one more stormy night to endure. What a night that turned out to be. At sunset Simon emerged from the corner he had been sleeping in all day, hopped around the cabin, climbed over me as if I wasn't there, and then clearly conveyed to me that he didn't think the accommodation was up to scratch and was keen to be on his way. (He stood on a cushion behind my head and actually pecked repeatedly at the hatch.) I explained that conditions were still less than ideal (horrendous) and that it would be far wiser to stay put, but Simon was determined. So I reluctantly opened the hatch a fraction and turned around to get my video camera to film his departure. By the time I had turned back, Simon had already made his burst for freedom and was gone. It was a heart-wrenching moment to see him go and I felt rather bereft. I had formed quite an unusual bond with the little guy. The second heartbeat was gone from the cabin and the long night awaited.

Later in the evening conditions intensified and soon they were the worst I had experienced yet. I fully expected the boat to capsize at any moment and didn't sleep a wink all night. This was partly due to worrying about Simon and partly because I was being tossed around nonstop while bracing for action if the boat did in fact roll. My recurring thought was, "Just hang in there, Pete (and Simon), it will be over soon!"

The storm abated at long last the following day. I could hardly believe it was over; there were times when I'd forgotten my own advice and believed it would never end.

As conditions improved steadily over the course of a couple of hours, I was in and out of the cabin like a jack in the box checking to see if the wind had swung enough to make rowing worthwhile. Eventually I felt I could get back on the oars; I was itching to get at it after six days of "rest". But first, before I could start rowing again, I had to retrieve the para-anchor – a problem. I pulled on the polypropylene floating retrieval line to collapse the parachute but it was stuck fast. Having somehow wrapped itself around the main parachute line, it showed no signs of giving, and I realised the only way to proceed would be to pull the fully inflated parachute from the oceans depths. This was not going to be easy – as far as I knew, it might not even be possible.

I stood on the side of the boat and tried again with all my strength to pull the retrieval line but there was no budging it. To make matters worse, the swell was still so heavy that, after I took up the slack on the line in a trough, it would scream out of my hands as the boat rode up to the next peak. I eventually hit on a plan. I managed to pull the boat directly above the parachute and started the process of hauling it in, using the descent into the troughs to take up as much slack as possible then wedging the line against the boat when it ascended. It became the ultimate tug of war between the ocean and me – a contest you want to avoid as often as possible. In my frustration and exhaustion I nearly gave up several times and considered cutting the rope as the only viable escape option to allow me to get going again. Slowly, painfully, inch by inch, after an hour of effort that seemed ten times that, I finally managed to get it out. In the weeks ahead I would give thanks many times over for the fact that I didn't cut the para-anchor away because, having used it only once on my first crossing with Bill, I would have to use it repeatedly this time around.

Besides the time wasted and energy expended, the huge downside to the para-anchor debacle was the damage it inflicted on my hands. The one redeeming opportunity that the storm presented – six days' rest for my blisters and tendonitis – was almost entirely negated in a matter of minutes, with the rope tearing away the skin of my palms and sending my hands back to square one.

But even at this frustrating point, I was determined to remain upbeat about the general situation and so focused on the one amazing positive of the storm: I had had a buddy to keep me company who took up virtually no space at all.

During the storm I often spared a thought for the other crews, particularly the pairs and fours. They may not have been alone, but after a few days on top of each other in a tiny, sweaty, humid cabin, theirs would have been the opposite problem: no alone time. One crew in particular, Mick Birchall and Lia Ditton on *Dream Maker*, were a case in point. Mick's original partner had withdrawn from the race a couple of weeks prior to the original start date, and Mick, a middle-aged family man with a stable job, had managed to find a last-minute replacement in Lia, a 29-year-old professional sailor and artist – who happened to be a woman. Characters from entirely different worlds, the pair barely knew each other when they set off and they now had to spend a couple of months together on a rowing boat... An awesome challenge indeed! Not surprisingly they experienced rather a lot of conflict in the first weeks and their blog made for riveting reading. I was happy when I heard that Cliffy had advised them to use the Bill and Pete patented "90 minutes closer to Antigua!" technique, which apparently went down quite well.

The point is, for all my isolated, storm-ridden, rope-burned troubles, I had much to be grateful for. We are all going to experience turbulent times in our personal and professional lives. How we deal with these storms determines the kind of people we are or will become.

Remember that the storms will pass. See them as a test, and even an opportunity. If possible, find your Simon, even in the middle of the storm. Then use the situation to your advantage if you can, so that when the storm clears you are immediately up and running rather than left floundering in the wreckage. When it's all over and the clouds lift, you won't have just survived; you will come out rejuvenated.

MY DORADOS
Focusing on the positives

"Keep your thoughts positive because your thoughts become your words. Keep your words positive because your words become your behaviour. Keep your behaviour positive because your behaviour becomes your habits. Keep your habits positive because your habits become your values. Keep your values positive because your values become your destiny."
– **Mahatma Gandhi**

With the storm clearing after what seemed like an eternity, I was finally able to emerge from my cabin. I felt like a prisoner being freed after a ten-year sentence. It was the most exquisite relief to breathe the fresh salty air on deck and to know I was moving forward again. Every minute of delay meant an extra minute until I would see Hannah and Kim. Time to get cracking again.

Despite the euphoria of the moment, I couldn't afford to let my concentration slip. Conditions were still rough, with rogue waves appearing constantly; I had to be alert at all times. Although the white horses had subsided as the wind dropped, the swell was still enormous and would remain that way for some time. I also had to overcome the underlying psychological attrition that the storm had wrought.

The race organisers released the following communication on their website shortly after the storm abated, a good summary of its effects.

The fleet continue to suffer with adverse weather, having lost nearly 100nm between them through Day 24. With most of the fleet on para-anchor, crews become passengers in the ocean, and as a result over two thirds of crews have lost ground to the finish.

In conditions such as these where waves come from all angles, the boat moves and lists in a very unpredictable and unstable manner. This means that although competitors have learnt and accepted how to move around and get into or out of the cabins through the first few weeks of the race, Mother Nature then decides to throw a curve ball and disrupt these well-learnt processes. All of a sudden, getting into and out of a cabin becomes even more troublesome. Competitors will also be faced with terrible living conditions, far worse than the previous 3 weeks.

The risks of having a cabin hatch ajar have been well documented. Water in the cabin is one of the worst issues – taking away any possibility of comfort – and can obviously affect the electronic equipment onboard. But in leaving the hatch closed, cabin temperature will rapidly rise and create a very humid environment. Furthermore, being in even closer confinement, crew members will undoubtedly irritate and anger each other – competitors will need to learn to control and manage their psychological state even more to enable them to continue when the weather turns.

When in these conditions the morale of a crew can really plummet – especially as crews are unable to determine how other crews in the fleet are performing. It is really important to try and put the race to one side and focus on the challenge that they set out to complete. Crews can only control the controllable and make best use of all other skills and attributes in order to succeed.

I was rowing (predictably!) one morning after the storm when I heard a loud bang from the back of the boat. My concern was that something had connected with the rudder and damaged it, and I immediately interrupted my shift to investigate the noise.

It might have been another pilot whale or a turtle or even some ocean rubbish. There was nothing to be seen and the rudder appeared to be working as usual so, taking some comfort from the fact that the blow would have been amplified by the carbon of the boat and so perhaps was not as bad as it sounded, I got back on the oars.

A few minutes later I heard the same resounding bang, and for a second time I leapt up and hurried to the back of the boat to check the rudder. Again it seemed fine, but this time I could make out what appeared to be a couple of dorados swimming very close by. Could it be that they were responsible for the noise? I didn't think so at first because they would have had to hit the boat with some force, but I would later discover that they were indeed the noisy culprits.

Despite the interruption to my routine, I was delighted to see my new ocean companions because dorado are one of my favourite fish. Also known as mahi-mahi or dolphin fish, they are unmistakable, with a prominent dorsal fin that extends the length of the body and strikingly beautiful colouring: golden-yellow flanks and dazzling blues and green on their sides and back. They grow to a metre or more in length, can apparently hit speeds of 80km/h and eat everything from squid and crabs to mackerel, herring and, as I was to witness first hand, flying fish.

Dorado are extremely intelligent and are often believed to be the only fish that mate for life. The sexes are easily distinguishable – the male has a bulbous forehead like a mini sperm whale – and should you catch an adult dorado, so the legend goes, its partner will almost certainly come up to the surface with its doomed mate and lurk around anxiously until the situation resolves itself one way or the other. They are also fantastically good eating fish – though I abstain, and will do so forever more; you'll see why – which make them a great favourite with fishing enthusiasts. Sadly, this fact also results in many a tragic ending to fish romances…

(Equally sadly this great legend is untrue; it seems that dorado just like to hunt in pairs or small schools, and fishermen will often hook a second or even third dorado once they've caught one.)

I was aware there had been fish living under the boat prior to the storm because I had seen them, usually a couple of small tuna, when I dived in to give the hull a scrub. This came as no surprise: you would expect to find fish there, as part of the marine life that congregates under almost any substantial floating object in the open ocean – initiated by the pesky goose barnacles I was so keen to get rid of. Once barnacles stake their claim, molluscs and weeds can quickly follow. Tiny worms and crustaceans then appear, followed by small fish to feed on them and larger fish to feed on *them*. In the course of a week or so your boat and the water around it becomes a slowly moving marine ecosystem.

This is why a castaway on a raft or lifeboat who possesses a little bit of sea knowledge and perhaps a fish hook or two (or even an empty container with a hole in it) can survive without onboard supplies for many months at a time. In January 2014 José Salvador Alvarenga, a fisherman from Mexico, washed up in the Marshall Islands in the northern Pacific Ocean, claiming to have spent 13 months adrift in an 8-metre fibreglass boat after being blown off course by a storm and suffering engine failure. He had survived the 10,000-kilometre journey, he explained, by eating raw fish, turtles and birds, and drinking rainwater. Though his companion died after four months at sea, the ability to harvest that much food from the ocean is well documented and entirely plausible. In fact the veracity of his story has been queried because Alvarenga appeared *too* healthy.

Much larger predatory fish such as sharks, marlin, sailfish and wahoo are, of course, attracted to the dinner that tags along beneath your boat, which is why it's always wise to have a good look around before taking a mid-ocean dip. Though I didn't spot any sharks on this crossing, I was particularly wary of marlin, which are notoriously aggressive and which I had seen hunting tuna more than once.

On one occasion, after hopping overboard to rescue a sunfish trapped in a floating plastic container, I nearly dirtied myself when I was confronted by a large marlin that swam within three metres of me. Reluctant to prolong the encounter, I clambered back on deck as soon as my rescue mission was complete. My awareness of the marlin danger was further heightened when Kim relayed an incident that Paul Williams on the four-man boat *Limited Intelligence* had blogged about. Not long after passing the halfway mark, with two rowers on the oars, the following happened.

One of the larger waves was building behind us, we could just feel it start to give the boat a helping push. Suddenly a loud and violent thud under the boat snaps Andy and me out of whatever we're thinking. We have hit something or it has hit us. The back of the boat instantly starts to lift. It is not being lifted by the wave, it is being lifted by whatever is beneath us. My immediate thought is that a whale has just tried to surface under the stern of our rowing boat. The back of the boat continues to lift, not quite out of the water, but the keel is very close to being exposed to air for the first time since she was lifted into the water in La Gomera. The forward momentum of the boat, accelerated slightly by the wave, then pushes us over the beast. We can feel and hear our steal rudder being dragged over something much tougher than water. As we drift clear of the animal we can see behind the boat something maybe 3.5 meters long and 2 metres wide writhing just below the surface of the water.

Having checked for rudder damage, they rowed on, slightly mystified but assuming they'd hit a whale. Forty-five minutes later Paul noticed a problem with their water desalinator, which in turn led them to discover what they at first thought was a tusk or whale rib sticking through the keel of the boat in the hatch in the aft cabin. They quickly realised it was a marlin's bill, and so had a more likely explanation for the incident.

The marlin had either mistimed a run on one of the many smaller fish we had seen it chasing previously, or for some reason it had attacked us directly. Atlantic Blue Marlin can grow to a significant size and weigh over 1,000kg. This fish must have run at the boat at some speed from almost vertically below. The force of it hitting the bottom of the boat pushed its bill through the skin of the boat (a fibreglass and foam composite) and lifted the stern of the boat high in the water. The forward momentum of the boat with the fish now perpendicular to our direction of travel then broke the bill from the fish.

Fortunately, the bill had made a very clean hole through the bottom of the boat, which resulted in less leaking than they might have expected, and the *Limited Intelligence* team turned out to be possessed of sufficient intelligence to fix the problem mid-ocean. Leaving the bill in place as a plug – rather than removing it and risking overwhelming their hand-held bilge pump – they tried using epoxy putty and then marine sealant to stop the inflow of water. For the remainder of the race they had to pump out water at regular intervals, but it was a good enough job to see them to Antigua.

And so, even though the marlin came off second best in that case, I was understandably wary of the big fish.

A few days after I first noticed a few dorados around my boat, it occurred on me that it was the same fish I was seeing every time. A dorado family had moved in. We started getting friendly. At the end of each rowing shift, when the heat was unbearable, I would attach myself to the safety line and jump overboard to cool down. Delighted to see me, the dorado family would immediately join in for a sociable group swim. There were six of them; three pairs, I assumed. They were magnificent fully grown specimens, more than a metre long and perhaps 15 kilograms.

Each time I joined them for a dip they would swim a little closer to me, becoming accustomed to me and comfortable with my routine. Call me crazy, but in my bizarre state of loneliness and craving interaction with a living thing of any kind, I was certain that they were warming to me. I was convinced, in fact, that they liked me!

Soon, in addition to our regular swims, my dorado friends began leaping out of the water at sunrise and sunset, greeting me in the morning and saying goodnight when they went to bed. There is no doubt in my mind that they were intent on making eye contact with me when they did this – with just the one eye, of course, given the fish shape of their faces – and these regular high fives with my dorados became one of the highlights of my daily routine. I realised I was not going completely insane and imagining myself communing with fish when I discovered that they would start jumping in the morning before I got up and only relax into their usual fish routine once they'd seen me emerge from the cabin. On occasion, when I was resting during these times and was too tired to get out on deck, they would swim up to the boat's rudder and bump it repeatedly. As soon as they saw me and were satisfied I was still alive and well, they would stop.

I was immensely comforted, particularly at night, by the knowledge that my dorados were keeping me company just a few metres from the boat. Although I usually couldn't see them, there were nights when the ocean was full of phosphorescence and if anything disturbed the surface it lit up in a spectacular display of luminous green. I would often see the reassuring brilliant green outlines of my dorados dancing beneath the waves just under my oars.

By day, I would watch my companions hunt, and towards the end of the race, when I was nearing land, I was privileged to see them operating in tandem with frigate birds.

At first light one morning, I heard an unusual sound – a bird call. One of the fascinating traits of mid-Atlantic sea birds is that they make absolutely no sound. They fly silently in the troughs of the swells looking for food near the ocean surface. It's quite eerie, really. Closer to land, more species of birds appear. The call I had heard was from a frigate bird, a remarkable creature with iridescent black feathers and a deeply forked tail that looks rather like an avian dinosaur. With the largest wingspan-to-body-weight ratio of any bird, it lives a predominantly aerial existence, able to stay aloft for more than a week and landing only to roost or breed on trees or cliffs.

I eventually spotted two individuals circling high above me like black eagles hunting. It was my first sighting of frigates, a good sign because it meant the finish line was approaching. I could not have predicted I would soon be witness to my own private nature display worthy of a David Attenborough documentary.

Frigate birds, also known as pirate birds, are so called because of their propensity to rob other seabirds of their catch, using their speed and manoeuvrability to outrun and harass their victims until they either let go of their prey or regurgitate their stomach contents. More often, though, frigates catch their own food. Unable to swim or enter the water, they snatch prey from the ocean surface using their long, hooked bills, catching fish, baby turtles and the like. As I was about to see, this is quite a sight and they have quite the appetite.

It didn't take long to get to see them in action. My dorado family would regularly hunt from the safety of my hull and I especially loved to watch them chase down flying fish. It was spectacular to watch. They would dart out from under the boat at top speed and within seconds flying fish would begin frantically exiting the water in an attempt to evade capture by "flying" (effectively gliding). They were extremely fast and I was always convinced the dorados would never keep up. But, swimming just below the surface on their sides looking up and keeping a beady eye on their dinner, they were smart enough to predict where their prey would land. As the flying fish ran out of lift and touched down, the dorados would pounce and there would be a violent splash before it returned smugly to the boat a little plumper than before.

But my friends had competition. Now, whenever the harassed flying fish leapt from the water to evade the chasing dorados, the frigates were ready to swoop. And swoop they did, gorging on kilograms of flying fish during the course of the day. They were so successful and consumed so much that I was sure the birds would eventually tumble from the sky – but they seemed insatiable. The poor flying fish stood no chance at all: death was waiting for them from above and below as the frigates and dorados closed in.

My dorados had to work a little harder for their supper now, but I was delighted by the competition between fish and bird, which provided me with several hours of *National Geographic*-quality entertainment.

For six weeks, from that first bump of the rudder until the last day of the race, I interacted daily with my dorados. At the risk of sounding as if I need prolonged and expensive therapy, I knew without a shadow of doubt that they cared for me. We developed a meaningful and very satisfying relationship, which reminded me that the link between animal and humans is as strong as ever if we open ourselves to it. Sadly, we are so insulated by modern civilisation that we have largely lost our ability to interact on this level.

On the last day of the race, at 6am, I jumped off my boat for the last time to say farewell to my fish family. They had followed me from the mid-Atlantic all the way to Antigua. We swam together for 15 minutes and I explained that our time together had come to an end. It was an emotional goodbye!

Even today I think of my dorados often and I will be forever grateful for their companionship during my solo row. Whereas Simon the storm petrel had been a blessed distraction during the intensity of the storm, the dorados uplifted me daily over a much longer period that saw my energy and spirit being steadily sapped. Their presence gave me something other than myself on which to focus; something inherently positive. They were the extra heartbeats under the boat that provided me with a comforting sense of security. Of course, they would have been unable to assist me in any way in a storm or a hazardous situation – and no, I couldn't speak fish by the end of it! – but they were an invaluable part of my routine and they did wonders for my morale.

I have attended many inspirational talks delivered by individuals who have survived horrifying situations or incidents against all odds; people who have all endured great hardships and emerged stronger rather than broken. Most of them speak of consciously identifying and then focusing on something positive as part of their survival strategy. Like them, I realised it was better to focus on the positives during a difficult situation than feel sorry for myself and disappear down a negative spiral of despair. Self-pity is the least useful of all emotions, I believe, and I would reinforce this notion while aboard *Nyamezela* by using a brilliant DH Lawrence quote as a mantra: "I never saw a wild thing sorry for itself. A small bird will drop frozen dead from a bough without ever having felt sorry for itself."

Given the animal allusion, it was perhaps appropriate then that my dorados came to be my enduring positive. Along with other wildlife encounters and chance rendezvous with boats and ships, I chose to be inspired by them rather than demoralised by other factors beyond my control such as pain, exhaustion, loneliness and bad weather.

There is no doubt in my mind that, even with the best boat, gear and credentials, you cannot set off to row across an ocean – or achieve anything of meaning – without the right mindset. By focusing my mind on the good things around me, I boosted my chances immeasurably.

Rain squalls could either be grumpily endured because they were accompanied by rough seas and high winds and left you wet and uncomfortable, or they could be seen as a great fresh-water shower opportunity, an easy option for collecting drinking water and an opportunity to cool down after an intense rowing session in the tropical heat.

Similarly, six dorados using your boat as a temporary home could just be some dumb fish bumping the boat and getting in the way, or they could be a once-in-a-lifetime opportunity to commune with nature in a way you could never have imagined.

The choice is yours.

A NAKED CALL
Making the move from external discipline to self-discipline

"In reading the lives of great men, I found that the first victory they won was over themselves... self-discipline with all of them came first."
– Harry S Truman

One of the harshest challenges a trans-Atlantic rower faces while at sea in his tiny open rowing boat is dealing with relentless exposure to the sun. Due to race regulations that prevent the erection of any kind of shelter or awning, which could potentially function as a sail and thus provide an unfair advantage, neither *Gquma* nor *Nyamezela* offered the barest amount of shade on deck. As a result, when I was not in the (blisteringly hot) cabin, then I was constantly and simultaneously being exposed to direct sunburn and reflective burn off the sea (as well as windburn). Under the circumstances, the right hat is absolutely essential.

From the pairs crossing with Bill, I had come to understand just how important a comfortable, effective hat is, and it was one of my missions to source the perfect headgear before my solo attempt. I was accordingly delighted to find a white, very wide-brimmed cricket hat at a local sports shop that I was sure would serve me well.

As you can imagine, there is a lot of time to think when you're an ocean-rower with no-one to talk to, the upshot of which was my invention of various mind games to keep me entertained. A favourite was coming up with pun-worthy names for my essential equipment. Thus my autohelm was christened "Helen Tiller" after Helen Zille, leader of South Africa's Democratic Alliance. My life raft became "Rubber dinghy Sithole" after Ndabaningi Sithole, teacher, clergyman and intellectual leader of the Black Nationalist movement in Rhodesia, later Zimbabwe. My bucket, used for ablutions of the worst kind, was proclaimed "Julius My Emmer", *emmer* being the Afrikaans word for bucket and Julius Malema being the idiotic, trash-talking leader of the ANC Youth League at the time. Considering the bucket's contents, I was particularly proud of that one.

By contrast, my much-loved cricket hat was named "My-Hat-Ma Gandhi" after Mahatma Gandhi, champion of peace and father of the Indian Independence Movement. I cherished My-Hat-Ma and was grateful for his efficient and comfortable sun protection every time I put him on my head. You can't underestimate the importance of a small detail such as this when it is extrapolated, day after day, over the course of an endurance expedition.

One tragic morning, as I was settling into my rowing seat for a shift, an unexpected gust of wind blew My-Hat-Ma off my head and into the sea. Instinctively I leapt up and dived after him into the water. Losing the perfect hat – my friend! – would be a disaster. But as I hit the water I cursed myself, realising I had not attached myself to the safety line before jumping overboard. When I surfaced from the dive I turned back to check on the boat and the cold realisation of what I had done ran like a shiver through my body. *Nyamezela* had already been carried a good 15 meters downwind and was moving quickly. I was momentarily torn. I was desperate to retain my hat, but being separated from your boat in the middle of the ocean is a rower's worst nightmare – and a death sentence. (Being hit by lightning and getting so sick that you can't communicate are two of the others.)

Once I'd realised the extent of the danger, the choice was simple. I turned back and swam for safety with all my strength, leaving my beloved cricket hat to float gently into oblivion. I worked really hard to catch the boat, and after clambering back on board I had to sit on the deck for a few minutes to regain my equilibrium. I was stunned and angry with myself for my carelessness. In a matter of minutes I had broken almost all my golden safety rules.

I had not attached myself to the safety line as I exited the cabin.

I had not fastened my hat to my head with the lanyard.

I had not scanned around the boat for sharks, marlin and other threats before jumping overboard.

I had not attached myself to the swimming line that I had set up on the deck for just such occasions.

My-Hat-Ma Ghandi had paid the ultimate price for my carelessness. For a moment I understood the relationship between Tom Hanks's character and "Wilson", his volleyball, in the film *Castaway*. My-Hat-Maaaaa!

What would I do without my perfect hat? Fortunately I had a spare, but it could never fill My-Hat-Ma's shoes.

I realised that a severe pep talk was in order. I had been alone at sea for a number of weeks and had become blasé about certain critical safety and discipline issues. One thing I was fastidious about was sticking to my shifts; I never allowed myself to sleep in and miss the start of a shift, and I never stopped a shift early, even by a second. This was non-negotiable if I wanted to achieve the goals I had set for myself. But I had started slipping in other areas. What would be the point of my rigid shift schedule if I allowed myself a colossal safety blunder that jeopardised the race, or even my life?

As I rowed my next shift – in my second-rate hat – I thought long and hard about discipline. In particular I contemplated the difference between external discipline and self-, or internal, discipline. I came to the conclusion that there is a vast difference between the two.

When Bill Godfrey and I raced together on *Gquma Challenger* we rowed in shifts of 90 minutes on and 90 minutes off 24 hours a day, seven days a week for 50 days. Although it took tremendous discipline to do this, my presence helped Bill and his helped me. Ten minutes before the end of every shift, one of us would wake up the other with an information update and a barrage of motivational chatter, including our "90 minutes closer to Antigua!" mantra. Pressing the snooze button was not an option. The resting person *had* to vacate the cabin to make way for the one coming off shift. The rested person *had* to take up the oars and row – because he would have been assaulted otherwise.

Although it was tough for me to step up to the oars every hour and a half to do my duty, the discipline required to do it was enforced by someone else. Hence, external discipline. This is why the idea of training under a coach or with a buddy is often a good one; it's much easier to get up at 5am and go running in the rain if your coach or training buddy is waiting for you (or rather it's harder to *not* go). It's much easier to work on your report until 2am if your boss is waiting to see it first thing the next morning.

Internal discipline, or self-discipline, is another matter.

Try to imagine yourself on *Nyamezela* at 3am in the middle of the ocean, with your next shift scheduled to start. It feels like your last shift just ended and you closed your eyes barely a minute ago – and now the alarm is going off insistently. It's raining outside and waves are breaking over the boat. Your hands are riddled with blisters and callouses and tendonitis, and ache at the mere thought of picking up an oar. Your bottom, covered in pressure sores and salt rash, does likewise at the thought of sitting on a wet, hard seat for an hour and a half. You are achingly lonely, exhausted and hungry (always hungry!). There is no coach or teammate to harass you. No-one will ever know if you press the snooze button or even if you decide to skip the entire shift. It's just one shift, after all, and your brain (despite its exhaustion) is offering compelling arguments for why this would in fact be a very good idea.

You certainly *can* press snooze or throw the alarm clock into the Atlantic if you want, but only if it's not your dream to win the race and perform to your absolute limit. And hell, you could probably do it once or twice and get away with it anyway... But you know that if you do, a small mental process will occur inside your head and the next time you're in this situation it will be that much easier to do exactly the same thing again. Each time it will be easier and easier to press snooze, and eventually your discipline and motivation will drain away. You have no choice, really, in that terrible moment at 3am, but to stick to your self-imposed rules, get outside into the rain and wind, and start rowing – and if and when things fall apart, your routine cast in stone is the thing that will actually keep you going.

This, then, is self- or internal discipline. It is you; just you. Only you will ever know that you have pressed the snooze button. Remember that it is not the mountain we conquer but ourselves. And when you do row that 3am shift in the worst possible conditions, there is no greater satisfaction than knowing you have pushed yourself way past the point that most people would be prepared to go, and that you are conquering your Eighth Summit

Barring weather-enforced breaks, I missed only one shift in the combined 126 days of my two Atlantic Rowing Races. I was driven externally in one race, internally in the other, and in both by an overwhelming will to accomplish what I'd set out to achieve – as a result, I managed to override the desire to press snooze and grab a few minutes of extra sleep every time. Even when I managed to miss a shift.

My one lapse happened towards the end of the solo row while I was passing through the final shipping lane of the crossing. I was at my most vigilant in the lanes because my experience had taught me that most ships' bridges are left unmanned. I know this because of all the ships that I saw and attempted to contact, perhaps one in ten ever responded to my calls. Of course, it is the rest shifts that are the most dangerous as a solo rower, as you cannot see approaching vessels and have to rely on the (pathetically soft) alarm of your Automatic Identification System to warn you of their approach. So you begin to listen rather for the deep rumbling sound of a ship's engine.

During the afternoon of Day 70, I noticed a vessel about 25 nautical miles away, which the AIS informed me was a cargo ship called the *Asian Grace*. Although we were both headed in the same direction, we were not on a collision course and she wasn't close enough to get a visual while I was on shift. Keeping track of her on the AIS, I noted, just before I disappeared into the cabin to rest, that she would miss me on my port side by about 15 nautical miles. This was a wide enough margin to feel comfortable and I calculated that at her current speed of 14 knots she would have passed me by the time I woke.

Deep into my rest, through the haze of sleep, I slowly became conscious of the thudding sound of an engine. At first it seemed to form part of my dream, then suddenly all my alarm bells rang at once, my brain screamed "COLLISION!", there was a flood of adrenaline and I scrambled frantically out the cabin.

An enormous bulk consumed my entire view. In my confusion I couldn't make out what it was. And then I looked up... and my perspective cleared.

I had been looking directly at the hull of a ship. It was the *Asian Grac*e – her name was clearly emblazoned on its side – and, a good 150-metres long, she had come to a complete stop just a stone's throw from *Nyamezela*.

I could see a crowd of people gathered on the wing of the ship's bridge deck. A number were dressed in white uniforms, presumably the ship's officers. They had clearly been trying to communicate with me, but with my VHF radio turned off to conserve battery I hadn't heard a thing. When I leant into the cabin and switched the radio on to channel 16 it immediately burst into life. The ship's captain had picked up my signal on their AIS system and, intrigued by the description of my boat – "Nyamezela: rowing vessel" – had changed course so they could come see for themselves what it was.

We then enjoyed a long and varied discussion, including the standard questions a cargo carrier might ask a rowing boat during a chance mid-ocean meeting: why was I doing the race, did I need any assistance, where was I heading, was I insane, was life at home so awful that this seemed like a good alternative etc. We also discussed the weather forecasts for the next week or so, as mariners do, and I found out a little about them. Like me, they were heading towards the Caribbean.

Suddenly, in the middle of the conversation, it dawned on me that I was stark naked. I must have looked utterly nuts with my huge red beard, wild eyes and skinny naked body with all-over tan, chatting away merrily in the middle of the ocean on a tiny rowing boat. The humour of the scenario was not lost on me and I started to laugh uproariously – confirming my insanity to all those aboard the *Asian Grace*, no doubt. The growing crowd on the bridge deck looked increasingly concerned and asked repeatedly if I was certain that I did not require any assistance. It was the most I had laughed for the entire journey, and it felt good.

The conversation ended at last with the ship's engines thudding once more to life, before the *Asian Grace* continued on her way, taking very little time to disappear over the horizon.

My mood swung wildly from the laughter and fun of my socialising highs to an abandoned and gloomy low, and I decided it would be best to rest again immediately and miss an entire shift of rowing. There was little pleasure in it. I felt so guilty about my lapse that I started the next shift 30 minutes earlier and rowed for two hours into the dark moonless night in the hope of achieving redemption.

Still, in retrospect one lost shift over close on 11,000 kilometres of rowing is pretty good going.

*

In progressing from a pairs crossing of the Atlantic to a solo crossing, it was obvious that my self-sufficiency and independence were going to be tested to the utmost. One of the greatest lessons that I learnt in the process was the difference between external and internal discipline and the importance of mastering the second to achieve regular success in our lives. I believe that if we can increasingly make that transition from external discipline to self-discipline then, not only will we be met with a greater chance of success, but we may even achieve greatness.

It is no easy feat; you don't have to remind me. That fact was brought home to me when I lost my cricket hat to a stray gust of wind and foolishly dived straight into the ocean after it. You can have discipline in one aspect of your processes, but it can so easily be compromised by a lack of it elsewhere.

After the incident, and my much-needed pep talk, I was far more conscious of sticking to the safety rules that governed life on board *Nyamezela*, and I managed to steer clear of any more near-disasters.

In the modern multitasking world, there are so many distractions – so many options, so many balls to juggle – that internal discipline is an increasingly valuable trait to possess. I still work hard on it every day of my life. I have not yet got it right – it is human nature to slip – but I keep trying.

ARAGORN OF DUBLIN
The importance of passion

*"The motivation to succeed comes from the burning
desire to achieve purpose."*
– John Pichappilly

The first five days of an expedition are usually the most difficult. The extreme and immediate change from normal life to the rigours of the expedition, new and uncomfortable living conditions and an entirely new routine are a huge shock to the system. This is the period when you or your team are most likely to drop out – because the conditions are far beyond what you expected, the team dynamics aren't working under pressure or the fear and discomfort of reality are simply unbearable. How can you endure this for another two or even three months? You've bitten off more than you can chew. Better to quit now.

I am always deeply relieved when the first week is over and my body and mind have (reluctantly) made the transition into the new routine. The correct mental and physical preparations are key to this; experience also helps. The new routine then slowly becomes old hat and, as tough as things are, life becomes constant and predictable. You knuckle down. This is what you've come to do. Barring any major challenge or disaster, things progress fairly smoothly, day after day and week after week, and you become convinced by the illusion that it's all fairly straightforward from here. You're confident. But as time passes, your mental and physical reserves are imperceptibly depleting, just a little every day, until suddenly an invisible line is crossed and a further crisis may occur. You realise how drained you are and again you are faced with the real possibility of giving up; now you will find out if the need to persevere runs deep enough within you.

March had arrived and I was now approaching my third month alone at sea. I was beginning to feel the effects of my dramatic weight loss and was increasingly aware that my energy levels were deteriorating. During the day I was still motivated but my resolve would suffer as night fell. The lowest ebb was inevitably at 3am in the pitch darkness, the last shift before sunrise. I saved my daily ration of two sachets of 3-in-1 Enrista coffee for the preparations for this hellish shift, and the caffeine would at least ensure a certain level of alertness for the first 45 minutes or so. But as it wore off and exhaustion overwhelmed me while I was being tossed from side to side by the wind and waves, oars painfully clubbing my skinny shins and femurs, I would be filled with despair. I would fall asleep slumped over the oars or begin to hallucinate in a semi-conscious state, imagining that I was in a shopping mall or pulling up at a petrol station. Sometimes I would look at the compass that had guided me for weeks and have no idea what it was. As I clawed my way back to consciousness, it would dawn on me that I was in the middle of the ocean rowing a tiny boat and I would be overwhelmed by the insanity of what I was doing. There were a million valid and acceptable reasons to give up on this foolhardy expedition, and the temptation to throw in the towel was overwhelming.

My hands won't make it.

I will get septicaemia and die because of the sores on my buttocks.

The wind will push me north of the finish line, which will mean I will miss the finish line and be disqualified.

I am going to run out of food and supplies.

I'm being irresponsible putting my family through all this. It's my duty to stop!

My negative thoughts could be very convincing during these

143

early morning moments of doubt, and it was now that my fear, pain, exhaustion and desire to give up would be weighed against my passion for what I was doing and my desire to succeed. Our ability to endure great hardship is directly proportional to the amount of passion we feel for achieving the particular goal we have set. If the pain and the hardship outweigh the passion to succeed, the argument for giving up becomes impossible to ignore. So passion becomes one of the most critical keys to success.

Modern use of the word "passion" tends to link it mostly to romance and love affairs, and to some extent is has become frivolous, losing much of its original meaning and power. Derived from the Latin word *to suffer*, I like to think of passion as a burning, overwhelming, urgent, often irrational *need* to see something through to its conclusion. In this sense, the notion of suffering for your passion makes sense. You should never embark on a difficult goal unless you're convinced by your passion to achieve it, and thus your ability to endure through hardships for it.

An American writer, Christian Nestell Bovee, aptly summarised the kind of passion to which I am referring:

"Genuine passion is like a mountain stream; it admits of no impediment; it cannot go backward; it must go forward."

This particular brand of passion will not only assist you through the first five days of the race, it is eventually what you will survive off at 3am when you're 50 or 60 days in. No-one can endure extreme and prolonged pain, exhaustion and fear unless his or her passion outweighs absolutely everything else. This is a good thing in many ways, but there is no doubt that the line between heroically finishing what you have started and being an idiot can become very blurred. At what point does it become

144

foolhardy to press forward? Is it true that the only people who are clear about where the edge is are the ones who have gone over it?

By 6 March, with 560 nautical miles left to go, a welcome north-easterly had finally arrived to push me in the right direction, rather than the south-easterlies the entire fleet had been experiencing.

Having been frustrated for so long, I welcomed any distraction that might come my way. Turning these moments into positive events to focus on and re-energise my enthusiasm was critical, a theme already covered in "My Dorados". I took great comfort in the presence of my dorado family, something I was consciously grateful for, but I was always looking for a new diversion.

One morning, I noticed that a school of small yellowfin tuna had joined my dorados under the boat – the perfect opportunity to take my mind off the harsh realities of life and hook myself a little sushi. Despite the ready supply of fish beneath our keels, fishing is not a regular activity for rowers because of the time and effort involved. Terminating (not my forte!) and then preparing a thrashing slippery tuna on board a constantly rocking boat with limited surface space is a particularly drawn-out and messy affair. I had also been reluctant to fish, as I ran the risk of catching one of my dorado friends, something I had in fact done a week earlier before meeting up with Richard and Steven on *No Fear*. Given my situation, however, I decided that the fun (and protein) was worth the gamble. If I caught one of my dorados in error I would immediately release it, as I had done before.

Using a handline configured through a speargun bungee-cord, I ran a feather lure off the back of the boat. The feather lure doesn't create as much drag as other lures and thus slow down the boat, and the bungee cord allows for give when the fish strikes so I wouldn't have to man the line. Before long, a tuna took the bait and after a five-minute handline battle I landed a beautiful 5-kilogram specimen. Fantastic! What came next, however, was more mind-bending than fantastic. Having grown so comfortable with my dorados during the course of the race, I found the act of dispatching their fishy friend quite troublesome, particularly on a constantly rocking boat without the recommended equipment. To compound things, the process turned into something of a sensory overload. An interesting phenomenon common to people who spend long spells in environments without much colour variation is their reaction to sudden exposure to different bright colours. In my case, I had become used to an infinite variety of blues, whites and greys while out on the ocean and the shock of the bright red tuna blood spreading all over the place was almost overwhelming. How, I wondered, could one fish produce so much gore? (I would be exposed to the same phenomenon in Antarctica.)

Once I had mentally processed what was going on, the positive energy returned. Laid out before me was the freshest sashimi a man could eat and a brilliant source of protein for my fatigured muscles. Out came the wasabi, lemon juice and chopsticks, brought along for this very purpose and as yet unused, and I tucked in. My mood quickly lifted.

As if the tuna-induced excitement hadn't been enough to motivate and nourish me, the next day brought further surprise – and treats. I had just finished my midday shift and was sitting at the coolest spot at the back of the boat on the rudder inspection hatch making a sat-phone call to Kim, when I noticed an odd shape on the horizon. As I was in a shipping lane I had to be constantly vigilant for passing ships, but this was no ship. I said goodbye to Kim and hurried over to the Automatic Identification System, which informed me that a yacht named *Aragorn of Dublin* was 20 miles due east of my position. The curious shape I could make out had to be its spinnaker.

I put out a call on my VHF radio, and somewhat surprisingly got an immediate response from the yacht. Despite a pronounced Irish accent, I was able to establish from the skipper of the yacht, Patrick, that he and his wife, Catherine, and a crewmember,

Neil, were on their way from the Cape Verde Islands to Antigua. They were excited to have identified me on their AIS and were hoping to say hello on the way past. Unfortunately, because there were only three of them on board, and they were trying to make up for lost time due to the unfavourable winds we'd all been suffering, they weren't going to drop their large spinnaker and hang around. I was disappointed – it would have been wonderful to chat to someone for a few minutes – but I could well understand their frustration with the weather.

For the duration of my next shift I could see *Aragorn's* spinnaker in the distance as the yacht slowly closed on me. It was immensely comforting to know that there was human life nearby, a blessed break from the completely empty horizon and nothingness I was used to.

After my subsequent rest, by which time *Aragorn* was really close, I made contact again. Patrick informed me that, though their AIS had identified *Nyamezela*, they couldn't physically see the boat and, not wanting to miss me as they sailed on by, could I reveal my position. Excitedly I pulled out my flare kit. Different coloured flares are used for different scenarios and I had to be careful to use the right one. Red is for emergencies while white is used for warning or location signals. If a ship is bearing down on you and you want to avert a collision then the white flare goes up. If you're sinking or in trouble, then it's the red. Had I mistakenly used a red flare to signal my position to *Aragorn* and another ship in the distance saw it, it would be obliged to come and investigate the emergency.

I shot off my white flare and the radio immediately came alive again. They had spotted me and would be with me in a few minutes. As they approached I could see what they meant by a large spinnaker; it was huge and would have been very cumbersome to take down. I could hear their voices before I could see them, and then suddenly there they were, three of them clearly visible on the deck singing what sounded like Irish folk songs and punching the air with enormous mugs of beer.

Aragorn passed very close by. She was a sight to behold as she sailed so swiftly and silently past. (I so wished that I could move at that speed...) Patrick, Catherine and Neil interrupted their hearty singing to shout a few hellos and toss something overboard and then that was it – they were gone. It was all over in a flash and I felt as if I had experienced a sensory overload of people and colour and noise. For a moment I was almost bereft as I watched them disappear slowly into the distance, waving from the stern of the boat. I sat silently on my rowing seat for a few minutes, relishing the encounter and trying to take it all in.

Suddenly I remembered that they had tossed something overboard. Bobbing in the sea, it looked like a few empty 5-litre water bottles with a package attached to the top. I had a momentary dilemma. The Woodvale Atlantic Rowing Race was both unassisted and unsupported. This meant that I was prohibited from accepting anything from anybody during the race. Then again, I couldn't just leave a pile of plastic floating around in the ocean, so I decided I was within my rights to retrieve it. When I pulled it on board I could see that it did indeed have a package attached to the flotation bottles and when I ripped it open it I was stunned.

Neatly packed in paper inside a few plastic bags were six ice-cold beers, four raisin scones and a small container of butter, cheese and honey

I sat looking at the feast in complete amazement. I slowly opened a beer as if I were in a dream and sipped it reverently. I carefully prepared a scone and bit into it, imagining in that moment that I must have died and arrived unexpectedly in heaven. I ate every crumb of the scones and drank one beer, then I decided to keep the remaining beers as a reward for every 100 nautical miles I completed before the finish. I was at that moment about 500 nautical miles from Antigua, which meant I could immediately have another! I felt dizzy and light-headed from the overindulgence.

All the action of the past few hours was over. I climbed back onto my seat, took up the oars and followed after *Aragorn* into the setting sun. Just one day at a time. Just 500 nautical miles to go. Just a chip and a putt, really.

Kim's blog: All this mid-Atlantic socialising is really getting out of hand! Pete had a long chat on the radio with the yacht *Aragorn of Dublin* which was en route to Martinique. The yacht is skippered by Patrick with his wife Catherine and crewman Neil. Peter was concerned that they couldn't see him so he set off one of his white flares and was very excited that he had captured the event on film until he realised that he had failed to press record! (Sorry Moose!) The yacht came flying past *Nyamezela* with its spinnaker up – it will be in the Caribbean in two days, as opposed to Pete's two weeks (best case scenario!).

After *Aragorn of Dublin* had disappeared over the horizon at the exact point where the sun was so dramatically setting, I was thankful for how buoyed up I felt from my fleeting human contact. I was grateful beyond measure for my beer and scones, sent to me in my hour of need.

I so often encounter people who, after hearing of my crossings, will say: "Wow Pete! You've rowed the Atlantic Ocean twice, that must have been such *fun!*"

"Fun" is not exactly the first adjective that springs to mind, but crossing paths with *Aragorn* was certainly a fun encounter. Rather than describing the expedition as fun, I would say it was tremendously satisfying to know that I had found the strength to persevere when my body was screaming at me to stop and my mind was presenting a brilliant argument in support of my body.

Despite the relentless difficulty of my circumstances, somehow my passion for this expedition never wavered. Although there were entire days – even entire weeks – during which I struggled

149

through every moment, I moved from positive moment to positive moment, while beneath it all the burning desire to complete what I had started and to beat the Atlantic sustained me and managed to trump the desire to give up.

The knowledge that resolve and passion – when it is sufficiently strong – can carry you through the toughest times is deeply reassuring. That passion was the starting point for my solo crossing, and it's what saw me home in the end.

PART III

THROUGH ICE AND SNOW

In December 1911, Roald Amundsen led a team of five Norwegian explorers to the South Pole. It was the first time men had stood at the bottom of the world, and in so doing they had beaten the great British explorer Robert Scott in the race for this honour. It was a classic tale of triumph and tragedy, the climax of the Heroic Age of Antarctic Exploration, followed just months later by the death of Scott's team.

One hundred years later, I was given the opportunity to compete in the Centenary Race to the South Pole with the adventurer Braam Malherbe. It was an event like nothing I'd ever experienced.

RACING TO
THE SOUTH POLE

*"We took risks, we knew that we took them; things
have come out against us, and therefore we have no
cause for complaint, but bow to the will of Providence,
determined still to do our best to the last. Had we
lived, I should have had a tale to tell of the hardihood,
endurance, and courage of my companions, which would
have stirred the heart of every Englishman. These rough
notes and our dead bodies must tell the tale."*
**– from Robert Scott's "Message to the Public",
written in March 1911**

I first came to know about Roald Amundsen, Robert Scott and
their race to the South Pole as a teenager. Growing up in sunny
Windhoek, it was quite a stretch of the imagination to try to
comprehend the freezing, wind-whipped, ice-covered, snow-
driven conditions they had to endure.

Captain Scott's epic and ultimately tragic Terra Nova
Expedition, in particular, seemed otherworldly, as though he'd
taken his men to the frozen equivalent of hell on earth, only
to die 11 miles from his next food depot in late March 1912.
Seven months later a search party (led by the wonderfully
named Apsley Cherry-Garrard) discovered the tip of Scott's
tent projecting above the Antarctic surface and, once they had
dug into the ice and snow, his mummified body along with two
companions, Dr Edward Wilson and Lieutenant Henry Bowers.

Among their belongings they discovered Scott's "Message to the Public" (quoted in the epigraph to this chapter), a now-historic artefact that resounds with sadness and irony. He could never have known that his tale would indeed go on to stir the hearts of Englishmen, and also people around the world – including youngsters in Windhoek in the 1970s.

Scott's expedition was a story of stoic, stiff-upper-lipped courage against all odds that was destined to fail, and it includes one of the more fabled deaths recorded in history. Two weeks before Scott's own demise, the gangrenous and frostbitten Captain Lawrence Oates sacrificed himself for the sake of his team by deliberately walking out of their tent and disappearing into an Antarctic blizzard. Scott recorded his final words as, "I am just going outside and may be some time."

When news of the discovery of Scott's body got back to Britain three months later – the search expedition had to return to New Zealand before they could cable home – Britain mourned him and his men as they would royalty. King George V and the cream of British aristocracy attended a service to honour them at St Paul's Cathedral, presided over by the Archbishop of Canterbury. Thousands gathered in the streets outside.

Amundsen, meanwhile, returned home to tell his tale and see his name go down in history. Though it was not without its setbacks, his expedition was professionally planned and ruthlessly executed. He wore Inuit-style skins and used crack skiers and dog teams, sacrificing exhausted dogs along the way for food. Scott laboured in heavy woollen clothes and used ponies and manpower. Amundsen even had the luck of the conditions: decent weather and favourable ice where he landed in the Bay of Whales, allowing for a shorter overland journey. Scott's fate was sealed by unseasonably bad blizzards. In the end it was hardly a race; Amundsen arrived at the South Pole on 14 December 1911 and Scott five weeks later on 17 January the following year. "Great God!" he wrote. "This is an awful place for us to have laboured to it without the reward of priority."

Today Amundsen and Scott are perhaps better accepted for what they were: exceptionally courageous adventurers who pushed the boundaries of known exploration and science, and were subject to the whims of fate along the way. (The death of Scott's team has been described recently as "a tragic accumulation of circumstances".) There are (mostly) positives and (some) negatives to be drawn from both their examples, as you see fit. Often it's a matter of interpretation. Whatever you think of them, their achievements were remarkable.

In 2010, when I rowed the Atlantic on my own, one of the most memorable and inspiring audiobooks I listened to along the way was *Captain Scott* by Sir Ranulph Fiennes, narrated by the great Fiennes himself. As I toiled through the tropical heat, listening to this story of courage and disaster, I would be transported to the icy plains of Antarctica and feel thankful I was only rowing across on ocean. What, I wondered, was it like down there?

Back home after my solo row, I was in serious debt to Kim. Mainly it was "time debt", as she had held the fort for so long and assumed so many of the responsibilities of running the household. It was time for her to cash in her chips and head out on her own adventure.

In March 2011, a year after my row, she set out on an epic journey of her own along the entire perimeter of South Africa, which she called "Tri The Beloved Country" after Alan Paton's classic *Cry The Beloved Country*. "Tri", in this case, reflected the triathlon nature of her travels. Starting from East London, her plan was to run the length of our coastline to northern KwaZulu-Natal; mountain bike the inland borders between South Africa and Mozambique, Swaziland, Zimbabwe, Botswana and part of Namibia; kayak the 615-kilometre section of the Orange River that forms the rest of the border between South Africa and Namibia; then run the coastline from the mouth of the Orange back to East London. Her support team would consist of our au pair and general operations manager Kirsty Borbely, Hannah and me. It was an ambitious trip, to say the least.

About a third of the way in, Kim and I were mountain biking along the Botswanan border in the middle of nowhere near a farm called Temoerengone (really!). There had been no cellphone reception for days, but for some reason I had my phone on me, and when we reached the top of one of the many hills we were climbing it rang. Surprised to hear it ring in the first place, I was even more surprised to see that it was a call from Braam Malherbe. It had to be something interesting. Braam is an interesting guy!

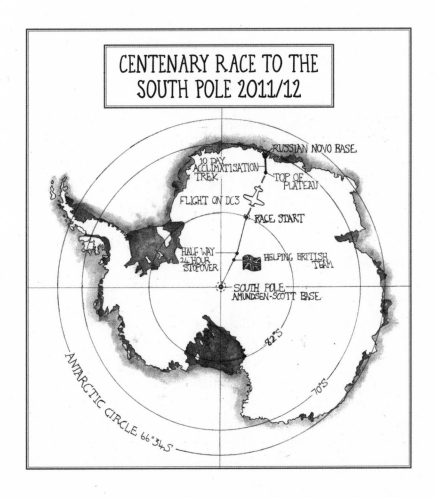

157

Like me, Braam is an adventurer and motivational speaker. He came to public attention in 2006 when he and David Grier became the first men to run the entire length of the main intact section of the Great Wall of China nonstop. A distance of more than 4,200 kilometres, it amounted to more than a marathon a day six days a week through sizzling deserts and freezing mountains. A unique and incredible feat.

I had met Braam just prior to leaving for the solo row. Along with David, he had run the South African coastline in 2008 and had a wealth of advice to help with Kim's trip, including all the right people to talk to to arrange the various permits we would need to run in certain areas. He had been a great help.

Now, after exchanging pleasantries on top of the hill, Braam got straight to the point. "Pete," he said, "I've just been asked to put a team together to represent South Africa in an international unsupported race across Antarctica to the South Pole, to commemorate the hundredth anniversary of Amundsen and Scott's race. Are you keen to join me?"

I grinned because it was a ridiculous question. There was no hesitation. "Braam, are you nuts? Geez, of course, I'm keen! I mean who in their right mind wouldn't be?"

I know that some people wonder about the rightness of the minds of people who row oceans and run thousands of kilometres, but for me this was a wonderful opportunity that I couldn't turn down. As Braam explained it, it would be a unique event covering close on 900 kilometres in the wildest place on earth.

"So when do we start?"

The start date was something of a concern. By the time I was due back home after Tri The Beloved Country, we would have little more than three months to prepare. My general fitness was decent, given that I was accompanying Kim on large sections of her trip, but it wasn't a lot of time for the specific training we needed. I had never cross-country skied in my life, let alone hauled a heavy sledge. In fact, the coldest temperature I had experienced was just -12°C. Antarctica in summer hits -45°C on a bad day, excluding wind chill.

Braam and I chatted for some time before I got a nudge from Kim. We had to be on our way if we were going to keep to our schedule for the day. As we cycled off together my thoughts drifted south to the coldest continent on earth. In a moment's conversation, Braam had planted the seed of a dream in my head. If I could find a way to take part, I knew there would be an amazing story to tell one day, but again I had no idea of what that story would be.

The remainder of Kim's expedition was extraordinary. I am certainly married to one tough woman. After 6,762 kilometres in 148 days we were back home at Sunrise-on-Sea in East London, and I was ready for a race to the South Pole.

Each of my Atlantic rows had taken a good two years to plan. Now we had just three-and-a-half months before we left for Antarctica. Time was of the essence. Luckily there was no boat to build and the sponsorship was taken care of – or so we thought – so it was more about preparing ourselves physically and technically to cope with the conditions that lay in wait. We needed to train to haul 90-kilogram loads on sledges and we needed to learn how to survive in extreme cold. I got stuck into the former immediately.

When you don't have fields of snow handy, the easiest way to imitate pulling a sledge is by rigging a tyre to a backpack and dragging it along a beach. It's a very effective system and soon I was hauling tyres for twenty kilometres at a time up and down sand dunes. I could feel the difference in my leg strength within the first week.

With Braam based in Cape Town, we spent hours on the phone planning logistics and talking race strategy. In late August, Braam and his girlfriend Hedda joined us for four days at the picturesque seaside village of Cintsa East, which has long beaches that were perfect for training. Our time at Cintsa East set the tone for our race, and it was a good one. There were other troubles to come, though.

Every time I start planning an expedition things seem easy and straightforward. Then, somewhere along the way, it turns into a monster. Or a monster gets in the way. In our case, the original sponsor that had approached Braam, a major car manufacturer, was now playing hard to get with the promised funds. We were due to head off to a polar-survival training camp on a high glacier in Iceland, which had been set up by the organisers, Extreme World Races. The cost of the camp was included in the race entry fee – problem being that the fee was yet to be paid.

At the same time I was trying to arrange for our race to be covered as a television documentary. Braam and I would film each other during the race but we would need a small crew to come out to the start and then meet us later at the South Pole. Having filmed both my Atlantic crossings, Moose was an obvious candidate, but he was busy on a documentary with Mike Horn. There was, however, someone else who I knew would just love this gig: Danie Ferreira, CEO of Urban Brew Studios in Johannesburg. I called him up and he jumped at the opportunity. Soon after, he flew to London to meet with Extreme World Races, and they agreed that Urban Brew Studios would film the entire race, making one documentary to cover the whole thing and another as a personal account of our story.

With our sponsorship still unresolved, Braam and I flew north to Iceland in early October. It was time for our polar survival training; a time for old dogs to learn new tricks.

This is how Ranulph Fiennes describes Antarctica in his recent book *Cold*:

"Antarctica is by far the coldest place on earth, with still-air temperatures of -88°C. In such temperatures mercury turns to solid metal, tin falls apart into granules, the flame of a candle becomes hooded by a wax helmet, and a carelessly dropped steel tube is liable to shatter like broken glass. [...] For humans in

Antarctica the danger is chiefly the wind. Each knot of wind has the effect on human skin of a drop of one degree in temperature."

He also notes that "a single stupid mistake made below freezing can easily cost a life or lives". Braam and I needed to learn how to avoid those mistakes, and how to ski well enough to make it to the South Pole.

When we landed in Reykjavik, we were surprised by the temperature. It was warmer than I expected, about 5°C. Iceland in autumn seemed quite pleasant. Those attending the course were booked into the Reykjavik Hilton for the first few days, where we would be covering all the theory of basic polar survival. How to avoid frostbite and how to treat it. Going to the toilet and making sure you zip up properly. Setting up your tent and other tent routines. Roping-up systems. Polar first aid and emergency operating procedures. And so on.

Being a barefoot khaki-broek South African who loves warm climates, I really had to focus on how to stay warm and survive in killer ice conditions. This was a world that was totally foreign to me. Happily I could relax a little when we moved on to navigational training; that was something, at least, with which I was well acquainted.

Once the theory was complete, it was time to head up to Langjökull, or Long Glacier, the second largest ice cap in Iceland. The higher we went the worse the conditions became; suddenly Iceland in autumn was not so pleasant any more. When we arrived at our scheduled position, a noteworthy blizzard was already raging, with 80km/h winds delivering a sleety snow into our faces. At -26°C it was by far the coldest temperature I had experienced to date. And yet we had been warned that the difference between -25°C and -45°C – what we could expect in Antarctica – is incomparable.

We immediately had a first thorough test of our tent-pitching skills in terrible conditions, after which we set about building an ice wall to protect the tent and our belongings inside it from the wind. Talk about a baptism of fire – or, in this case, a baptism of ice. It was vital, of course, because if your tent rips apart in Antarctica you would be in serious trouble. Braam and I then shared ours with a refreshingly unusual Kiwi, who was planning to trek the last 180 kilometres to the South Pole... with his family. We were now living among polar people...

Antarctica is, among other things, the windiest continent on earth. If you think Cape Town's Cape Doctor is maddening or you struggle with the regular gales in Port Elizabeth, they are nothing compared to a blizzard in a tent in Antarctica, with the wind screaming against the flaps so hard it feels as though it's blowing right through your head. Sleep is an impossibility. Our first night on Langjökull was good preparation for what lay in store, and it made our attempt at cross-country skiing the next morning all the more challenging. Not only were we learning to ski, but we were doing it while pulling manhaul sledges, or "pulks" as they are known. I will never forget leaning over my skis, checking all the bindings and thinking to myself, "I can't see further than five metres ahead, it's absolutely freezing and it's just six weeks before I start a race to the South Pole – here goes my first real skiing experience!"

Surprisingly, it went well. For whatever reason, I picked it up relatively quickly, perhaps because of my years of surfing. Skiing next to Braam for most of the time, I was really happy to see how comfortable we both were, in the conditions and on our skis. It was a great relief, as this had been a major concern. Our race would have been doomed if we couldn't crack skiing.

The session didn't last long, however, because the conditions were deemed too dangerous. Our instructor, who had been guiding people to the North and South Poles for more than thirty years, informed us that this was one of the ten worst blizzards he'd ever experienced, so we were pleased to escape back to civilisation – but it did get me wondering what we would do under similar circumstances in two months' time when we didn't have the option of taking refuge in the Hilton!

Besides manhaul skiing, the other important skills we focused on in Iceland were tent pitching (vital!), rope work and crevasse-rescue training. The initial part of the race would be an acclimatisation trek through glaciers that lead up to the Antarctic plateau at more than 3,000 metres above sea level. Navigating the crevasse fields on these glaciers is treacherous work, and if one of us took a bad fall and we bungled the rescue, survival was unlikely. The danger of the terrain was one of the reasons why we wouldn't be racing through this area. The other reason was the potential for developing altitude sickness if we ascended too quickly, a serious life-threatening affliction that had affected both the Scott and Amundsen teams a hundred years before.

By the time our short stint in Iceland was done, both Braam and I were feeling a lot more comfortable. I had enjoyed the training and felt ready for the cold of Antarctica. Deep down I knew we were going to be okay. I just needed to do some more ski training.

Back in South Africa our fitness training and logistics planning continued. We needed to find somewhere to get cracking on further long-distance cross-country skiing training and we needed to finalise the sponsorship problem, which still hadn't been resolved. It was becoming quite embarrassing, in fact, and playing on our minds. The mental processes you go through before setting out on any venture in life are critical to your ultimate success and this was proving to be a constant distraction, undermining our efforts.

Several deadlines passed before we escalated our enquiries, until eventually Braam's original contact at the car manufacturer got back to him. It was a no-go. They were pulling out of all sponsorships to focus exclusively on the Dakar Rally.

When Braam called to tell me the news I was completely blown away. *They* had approached Braam originally and now they were the ones quitting. I had sensed for weeks that things were not as they should be, but this was a hammer blow. It seemed far too late to find another sponsor for such a costly trip.

I called Danie at Urban Brew Studios to break the news. Like me, he was gob-smacked. What an anti-climax. All that training and preparation and anticipation for nothing. In Danie's case he'd flown to London to secure the rights to film the whole event and now the South African team's spot was in jeopardy. We needed to pull a rabbit out the hat.

In the end Danie was our saviour. Before the day was out, Urban Brew Studios had stepped in and rescued the situation. Next thing we knew, our race entry was paid and money made available for our next training trip. Unbelievable! Both Braam and I will forever be grateful for Danie's intervention.

The training trip in question was to Tignes in the French Alps, which offered snow and ice all year round on Grand Motte, a high glacier at 3,600 metres. Having co-hosted the 1992 Winter Olympics, it has a perfectly manicured 4-kilometre cross-country skiing track that was not only open (unlike most others in November), but perfect for our requirements. Freddy Louw, part of the film production team and filmmaker par excellence, joined us to film our training.

We arrived at our training area after a short underground and near-vertical train ride to the top of the mountain. The view from the top was spectacular and we stared in awe at the picture-perfect scene. I hadn't spent much time up on snow-capped mountains; I could get used to this. But it quickly became clear that we were ineptly kitted out. A group of 12 skiers arrived next to us – the two semi-clueless Saffers – looking very serious and professional, all suited up in Italian colours. It turned out they were the Italian cross-country skiing team, and we couldn't help but laugh at the thought of sharing a track with such pros. With our not-quite-10-kilometres of previous ski experience, this was going to be entertaining...

Braam and I decided to hang back for a few minutes to avoid embarrassing ourselves unnecessarily. Once the suave-looking Italians were almost out of sight down the track, we set off after them at a much more civilised pace. Sadly, it didn't take long for the first of the Italians to lap us, whizzing by as we laboured gracelessly on. We must have been quite a sight. A short while later, and to our horror, another squad of skiers arrived. This time it was the French team: *quelle horreur!* They were racing snakes of note. Now each time we were overtaken we could hear loud and incredulous comments between the skiers. I imagined their smug conversation (in a superior French accent) went something along the lines of, "Hey guys, check out these fools! Just take a look at their skis – they must think this is the South Pole or something. Could it be the Jamaican bobsled team? Haw-hee-haw-hee-haw!"

There was nothing we could do but battle on. Our speed was even slower than it might have been because our skis were designed for manhauling; they were longer and much sturdier than traditional cross-country skis to cope with the Antarctic terrain and to assist in pulling the heavy pulks. Despite our damaged self-esteem, we quickly started to improve both our speed and technique, in particular working on our "glide". This was largely because we were able to watch and learn from the annoying European pros.

Later on, the communal park on the edge of Tignes provided Braam and me with a perfect location for practising our tent set-up routine – or so we thought. First time around, we were delighted with our technique, congratulating each other that it had taken only eight minutes. We had hardly finished high-fiving each other when the local *gendarmes* appeared from nowhere to apprehend us for illegal camping. We tried to reassure them – in broken French – that we were being accommodated in a nearby villa and that we were just training for a race to the South Pole, but they couldn't work us out and didn't seem to care. We had to cease our activities immediately and *foutre le camp!* No further discussion. So much for our tent-pitching routine. We would have to save that for South Africa, where no-one bats an eyelid if you put up a tent in a park.

Minor embarrassments and inconveniences aside, the only real concern we had by this stage was Braam's health. He had been suffering from chronic bronchitis for several months and it started playing up again in France, no doubt exacerbated by the altitude and dry air – the same conditions we could expect in Antarctica. By the end of our time in Tignes, he was coughing so badly he had to stop exercising, and it worried me that he wouldn't be fit and healthy in time for the start of the race. Nevertheless, he remained upbeat. He had already defied major knee surgery and then doctor's orders by running the entire coastline of South Africa, so hopefully he would manage.

Back home again, the last few weeks of preparation turned into a frenzy of activity, as they tend to before a big expedition. I had conferences to attend, kit to assemble and logistics to sort out, all as publicity for the event mounted. Braam attended the COP 17 United Nations Climate Change Conference in Durban, where he addressed the audience and Desmond Tutu blessed us. Standing on the stage before thousands of delegates, he declared, "On God's behalf, we bless you. We pray that the holy angels will walk ahead of you, and behind you, and bring you safely home. Amen." Then, as they moved off the stage, he giggled and said to Braam, "That should do it – you will be fine now!"

The Minister of Sport then even included us in his year-end message, calling us "two extreme adventurers and environmental activists who will represent South Africa in the race to the South Pole", before wishing us good luck in "one of the toughest endurance races in the history of humankind".

Meanwhile, I was keen to spend some time with Kim and Hannah before I left. We planned a five-day road trip from East London to Cape Town, where the teams were meeting up for final race briefings, but our trip was cut short on day two when I received a call from the race organisers. The schedule was being moved forward. It was time to go.

One thing I don't enjoy is waiting for an expedition to start.

After being hurried to Cape Town earlier than planned, we then had to wait around for storms at our landing strip in Antarctica to abate. Having suffered a month of nervous anticipation in San Sebastián before the solo Atlantic crossing, at least this wasn't as bad. On 21 December 2011, three days behind schedule, we departed Cape Town International Airport on board an enormous Ilyushin Il-76 airlifter bound for the Russian Antarctic research station, Novolazarevskaya, known as Novo.

Flying in the Ilyushin was quite an experience. The interior was draped with the flags of the countries that formed part of the Antarctic Treaty and had research stations on the continent. As a cargo plane first and foremost, it had no windows and was packed with crates and drums of fuel. It was somewhat daunting sitting a couple of metres from dozens of rattling drums of jet fuel, with wires hanging loosely from the ceiling and no window view for distraction. At least it took my mind off what was waiting for us at the other end of the five-hour flight, I suppose.

There was a buzz of excitement when the pilot informed us we had an hour to go before landing and that we should start getting into our cold-weather gear. Kit on and sun block applied – bearing in mind the ozone-depleted Antarctic receives the most vicious sun on the globe – we readied ourselves for landing. I had until that moment never landed in an aircraft on ice. There are few pilots skilled enough to bring an enormous jet plane onto a runway constructed entirely from ice and, having always maintained I would rather jump out of aeroplanes than land in them, I would be lying if I said I felt entirely comfortable when the Ilyushin touched down and its engines engaged the reverse thrusters. After what seemed like an age, the big plane came to a stop on the ice.

"This is it, Braam!" I said. We gave each other a quick hug and shook hands.

We were in the Antarctic. Scott and Amundsen territory. I could hardly believe we'd arrived on the continent that is the last true wilderness out there – the highest, driest, coldest, windiest continent on the planet. It is the highest continent as a result of the huge inland plateau that forms the bulk of its landmass, more than three kilometres above sea level. We would be trekking up to it as part of our acclimatisation before heading for the pole, which is itself at 3,400 metres. And it is the coldest continent both because of its geographic location and because of this height; the higher you go, the colder you get. The coldest directly recorded natural temperature on earth is -89°C, recorded at the Soviet Vostok station on the Antarctic Plateau in July 1983.

Stepping out onto the airstrip, I was surprised to see what all the Russians unloading the aircraft were wearing: mostly it was just ski pants and boots, with a long-sleeve fleece and a beanie. It was amazing how they had adapted to the cold. And here were Braam and I, kitted up in polar gear from top to toe, looking like proper tourists.

The teams we were up against, meanwhile, all seemed to be made up of extraordinary people – no tourists among them that I could see. The Norwegians were pipped to win the race, eager to prove that Amundsen deserved his victory a century earlier, while the other hot contenders were British and hoping to prove otherwise. The Amundsen-Scott debate certainly had a long way to run. Besides Braam and me – representing South Africa as Mission Possible, as we'd chosen to call ourselves – there were three other teams of mixed nationality, including Dutch, Brits, Germans and another South African.

Together, we spent two days making final preparations at Novo, which is located on Queen Maud Land about 75 kilometres from the coast, and more than 4,000 kilometres south of Cape Town. It is manned all year round and can handle several dozen people at a time. We were lucky with the weather, with pleasant temperatures around the -10°C mark that allowed us to prepare out in the open rather than in the confines of our tent. Most welcome was the lack of wind, which we had been repeatedly warned about. Besides the hellish blizzards they create, Antarctic

PART III: THROUGH ICE AND SNOW

CENTENARY RACE TO THE SOUTH POLE, 2011/2

Training with Braam on the beach at Cintsa. We attached tyres to our backpacks to imitate the load of our sledges – but the climate was a little harder to match.

Our first instructions on polar survival at the Hilton Hotel in Reykjavik, Iceland.

Practical training on Langjökull (Long Glacier) in Iceland.
Setting up our tents in the raging blizzard was not an easy
task. Sleep was impossible.

Packing our food rations at the Russian Novolazarevskaya research station.
We had two days at Novo for our final preparations. Note the biltong supplies!

Working our way up to the 3,200m high plateau during the acclimatisation trek. Trekking on the plateau was spectacular.

Antarctic selfie,
Day 2 of the race.

In the first few days of the race, my face swelled, which I later discovered was a sign of altitude sickness.

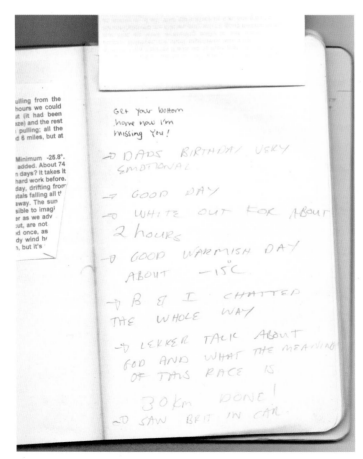

ulling from the hours we could at (it had been ze) and the rest pulling; all the d 6 miles, but at

Minimum -25.8°. added. About 74 n days? it takes it hard work before. day, drifting from tals falling all t' away. The sun sible to imag! er as we adv ut, are not d once, as dy wind h' n, but it's

Get your bottom home now I'm missing you!

→ DADS BIRTHDAY VERY EMOTIONAL

→ GOOD DAY

→ WHITE OUT FOR ABOUT 2 hours

→ GOOD WARMISH DAY ABOUT -15°C

→ B & I CHATTED THE WHOLE WAY

→ LEKKER TALK ABOUT GOD AND WHAT THE MEANING OF THIS RACE IS

30 km DONE!

→ SAW BRIT IN CAR

Missing out on important occasions is one of the downfalls of adventuring. This is my diary entry on 12 January 2012, my dad's 80th birthday. Note the papers pasted on the page; these are extracts from Robert Scott's diaries which I would read to compare his day 100 years before with ours.

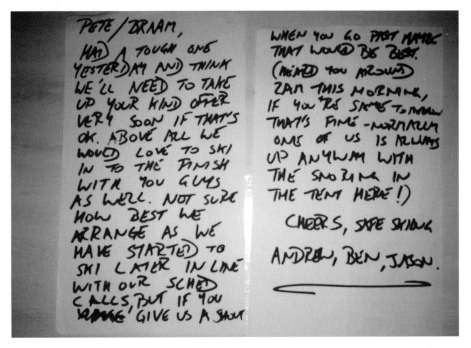

The letter left by the British Centrepoint team, accepting our offer to assist them. Braam and I took on the additional weight of the injured Andrew's gear, but the great company more than compensated for that.

Tent routine: I prepared food and melted ice for water in the cooking section while Braam set up the interior in the sleeping area and sorted out his chest and feet.

A few kilometres from the finish with our British
companions, Jason, Ben and Andrew. Note the
size difference of the flags. This was not planned…

Braam and me posing with the South Pole mirrorball – the moment of reward
for pushing through arguably the toughest endurance race in the world.

A world first. Ben holding a freshly overstruck silver coin. Minted in South Africa by SA Mint, they were flown to the South Pole specially, and we spent several hours overstriking them, the final process in their creation.

With the Urban Brew film crew (and a couple of Arctic Trucks) at Novo, before heading home. From left, Paul van Schalkwyk, me, Henri van Schalkwyk, Stafford Robinson, Braam and Danie Ferreira.

One of the perks of the adventuring job is the glamour-inducing weight losses we subject ourselves to... In trekking 888km to the South Pole in six weeks, I lost 13kg.

One of my greatest passions is using my stories to change the way people think about themselves and their businesses in my motivational talks.

Solo Atlantic Row

winds are renowned for whipping unsecured objects off to oblivion in the blink of an eye. If you're not careful, a loose mattress or jacket can skip off over the ice and be a kilometre distant in a minute, gone forever. For now, though, it was calm.

At this point, our greatest concern was Braam's chest. It hadn't taken well to the dry southerly air, and it was only going to get drier where we were going. I hoped it wouldn't deteriorate further. As the days passed and his coughing continued, he would constantly reassure me. "Don't worry, Pete, this is a case of mind over matter," he'd say. He kept coughing and I kept worrying, but he refused to let it get him down.

Finally, on a clear day with the wind now picking up, we headed off on the acclimatisation leg of the race, a 120-kilometre trek and three-kilometre ascent to the Antarctic Plateau. We had just 20 kilometres of skiing to get through on the first day, but it would be the furthest I had ever skied in one session. I was looking forward to acclimatisation because I was still learning the ropes!

We trekked and talked and told jokes, and in time got chatting with the other teams along the way. The Norwegians were well worth getting to know and we started picking up vital lessons from them, first from observing them in action and then in conversation. They explained to us how to control body temperature, and in particular the danger of sweating. Allowing sweat to pool on your skin and potentially freeze has to be prevented at all costs in low temperatures because it increases the chances of frostnip and then frostbite.

By the second and third days the enormity of the challenge ahead of us was there for all to see. We were back to Langjökull conditions, with a raging blizzard that had us holed up in our tent praying it wouldn't be blown away. What a way to spend another Christmas away from home... It wasn't easy creating a festive atmosphere in a tiny two-man tent with the Antarctic doing its worst outside, but luckily for us Kim had packed a brilliant selection of Christmas goodies, from tiny Christmas cakes and miniature bottles of Drambuie to a Santa Claus hat and a credit-card-sized book of laminated photos of her, Hannah, the cats and home. We were doing okay. A few of the other teams' tents were already torn but somehow ours seemed to be surviving. So far, at least.

The time delays caused by the blizzard on top of the earlier delays were putting pressure on the race organisers to get things going. Our planned start date for the race proper was 1 January 2012, but that was no longer going to happen. We needed more time to acclimatise and more time to reach the start. Various competitors were taking massive strain hauling slowly up the steep glacial slopes towards the Antarctic interior, and a general atmosphere of tension and negativity seemed to be building. Many of the teams felt they should be getting on with the race, not climbing mountains. In contrast, Braam and I were loving it. We felt privileged just to be there, doing what we were doing, and we felt stronger on the hills than on the flats, where our poor techniques were more obvious.

By the last day of 2011 we were at altitude, having arrived at the point where we were to be airlifted to the start of the race at approximately 82° south. Again there were delays, with bad weather preventing planes taking off from Novo, and we had to hunker down in our claustrophobic tents for two more frustrating days. I was really looking forward to being able to start ticking off the days and getting our butts to the Pole, but as with so many aspects of endurance events, it was a case of hardening our minds for the physical exertion ahead. As Braam would say: it's just a case of *mind over matter*.

We arrived at the race starting point late on 3 January, dropped off after a short flight in a refurbished Douglas DC-3 that landed on skis instead of wheels. Built in 1946, the plane was ideal for Antarctica, I was assured, and could be fixed with a screwdriver and shifting spanner. Nevertheless, my second ice-runway landing was about as nerve-wracking as my first…

Braam and I had our tent routine down pat by this stage. We set up quickly and prepared our sledges one last time before the real challenge began. With butterflies in the stomach and adrenaline pumping, sleep was going to be tricky. Weather conditions didn't help. It was almost exactly the middle of the Antarctic summer, when the sun never sets – rather it performs a full 360° circle in a wide arc above your head, which is quite something to witness and also an excellent navigational aid, but a sleep preventer of note. The constant howling wind that rattled our tent flaps all "night" long didn't help either.

I woke on the morning of the race as nervous and excited as I'd ever been before an expedition. After a short final brief from the organisers and a toast to Amundsen and Scott, the starter gun went off and the Centenary Race to the South Pole had begun. The other teams shot out of the blocks like it was a cross-country sprint at the Winter Olympics, leaving Braam and me in their wake. We turned to each other and exchanged what was to become our somewhat subdued Antarctic war cry. "Well?" I said. And he replied, "Shall we?"

And so we were at last on our way, setting off on this amazing journey across Queen Maud Land territory to the South Pole.

Braam and I recognised far in advance that it would be insane, and possibly even irresponsible, to try to match the other competitors right from the start. Rather, we would try a tortoise-versus-hare approach. South Africa may have a relatively sophisticated Antarctic research base – SANAE IV, not too far from Novo – but the polar heritage and skills certainly lay with the Norwegians and Brits, who had trained for years for this type of event and were well adapted to cold extremes. Braam and I had other expertise, but with no previous ice and snow experience and just three months' preparation, we had to be realistic. Our original intention was simply to survive all the way to the finish line, and to do it in a way that raised awareness of the challenges of climate change that lie ahead for mankind. If we were still standing at the end of it, it would be a win for us. As it turns out, this was quite an ambitious goal.

Braam: When Pete and I originally discussed the remote possibility of winning the race, I believed it would have been foolhardy, as the Norwegian team had been skiing all their lives and were determined to win for pride and love of their country and in honour of Amundsen. In fact, they even named their team "Fram", after Amundsen's ship. I suggested that we do it for a cause that may benefit others and the planet. He agreed, and the real message we decided to send out was that of the seriousness of climate change and, more importantly, what each of us can do to mitigate it. Given that Antarctica is the last great wilderness on Earth as well as a wonderful example of how everything on the planet is interconnected – the melting of Antarctica's ice ultimately affects us all – we coined the phrase "a race against time".

To symbolically show the seriousness of climate change, we approached the SA Mint Company in Pretoria and suggested that, as no coin had ever been minted on climate change, we overstrike the "90 degree South" seal on the first ever 1,000 coins on climate change – at the South Pole! The Mint agreed, minted the Centenary coins and flew them in a sealed metal case, with the two specially made privy presses for Pete and me, to the South Pole. The presses were aptly engraved "Centenary" and "Antarctica".

Every day all the teams had to check in by satellite phone with the race organisers. We would update them on our position and let them know how we were going, but they weren't permitted to divulge any information about the other contestants, including their whereabouts or wellbeing. We didn't know it at the time, but just five days into the race there were only three teams left in the running, and somehow Braam and I, the two barefoot khaki-broek South Africans, were one of those teams. (Although clearly we were not barefoot or khaki-broeked at the time!)

For the next two weeks, as we worked our way towards the halfway checkpoint and compulsory 24 hours' rest, Braam and

I settled into our routine. As I discuss at several points in these pages, routine is massively important to us while on expedition. Both of us believe in its value as a way to apply structure to our efforts and save time. At the end of a long day's trek it would be easy to become distracted and unfocused. We needed rest; the more efficiently we got things done, the more we could rest. When times are tough, routine also builds a sense (or illusion) that you have some control over things, and helps to rein in the doubts and fears that are inevitable in a contest of this nature.

We broke down our day into three trekking shifts of at least four hours each, split by two 15-minute rest periods. We aimed to cover a minimum of 30 kilometres a day. On a good day we could get that figure up to 40 kilometres; on a bad day it was a little more than 20. Because we were racing, we had to cover ground every day, no matter how bad the conditions. Unsurprisingly, the going was tough. One of the criticisms that Captain Scott posthumously faced was his decision to manhaul heavy sledges to the South Pole rather than use dogs like Amundsen, and it may well have contributed to his team's demise. Certainly taking ponies for a portion of his trip wasn't the greatest call, but manhauling has subsequently proven to be the most popular and effective form of transport for Antarctic explorers. As hard as it is, it is certainly more humane than killing your dogs along the way, an ethically troubling decision that Scott wouldn't countenance (he referred to it as "murder") and even the ruthless and hardened Norwegian icemen of a century ago found troubling and morale-sapping.

Whereas the physical effort of rowing the Atlantic had manifested itself in painful pressure sores and skin conditions and extremely debilitating hand injuries, trekking the Antarctic is all about pushing your legs and feet to their limit while protecting your extremities from frostbite. It is a constant battle to keep your hands and feet warm. Swinging your arms in wide circles forces blood to the fingertips, but there is no obviously practical solution for your toes, so you must constantly wiggle them to try to keep them alive. By the end of each day your inner boot liner is frozen solid with ice. Your face also becomes a high-risk area, and you must be constantly aware of the wind direction and temperature so that you can change your headgear to suit the situation. You must also apply sunscreen at all times, critical protection when there is no ozone above you, though completely counterintuitive when it's tens of degrees below zero.

At the end of the third shift we would make camp, erecting our tent as quickly as possible while the Antarctic winds did their best to slow us down. Having got the main structure up, it was my duty to secure the flaps and edges with heaps of snow and ice while Braam got inside and started preparing the cooking area in the front section of the tent. Again this saved time. With little space inside the tent, two people would simply get in each other's way; it was more efficient for one of us to get going inside as soon as possible while the other finished up outside. Braam would quickly get to work on digging a small hole in the cooking area, important both as a place to put our feet while cooking and to gather snow and ice to make water. Once I was finished outside, I would pass him the gear and food we needed from the pulks, before joining him inside. I would get cracking on cooking and preparing water for hot chocolate/tea/coffee, a very time-consuming process, while he set up the interior of the tent and got on to dealing with his injured toes and medicating his chest. Then it was mealtime together – inevitably freeze-dried rations along the lines of what I had eaten on so many previous expeditions – and perhaps a chat about the day's progress and life in general, before we hunkered down for the night.

Our brilliant Cape Storm goose-down sleeping bags were a wonderful refuge after each incredibly draining day. Settling in warmly when the outside air temperatures hovered in the -20°Cs and -30°Cs and later even -40°Cs was an overwhelming relief, even when sleep was hard to come by due to wind noise, our constant coughing and the never-ending sunshine. This last problem is perhaps more debilitating than you might expect. Being a light-adapted animal used to a daily light-dark cycle that regulates our flow of sleep hormones, humans are strangely affected by the permanently risen sun. Those who spend extended spells in Antarctica in mid-summer (or winter) without strict time schedules report shifting to different-length days, with sleeping patterns no longer dictated by the rising and setting of the sun. For Braam and me, sticking to a daily exercise schedule, it meant we probably averaged four to six hours of sleep a night, despite our overwhelming physical exhaustion. Braam insists that I snored but I didn't hear a thing!

We made it to the compulsory 24-hour stop at the halfway mark more or less in one piece and desperate for the enforced rest. It was time for us to recover, reorganise our sledges and get a few hours of extra sleep. Still camped there, we discovered, was the three-man British team, Centrepoint, which meant we were less than a day behind one of our more fancied competitors. Moreover, we found out that the two-man British team had already quit, having called in an emergency evacuation to Novo when one of its members contracted pneumonia from altitude sickness. We later found out he had come very close to dying. Two other teams were also out of the running, one pulling out on the back of ill health, equipment failure and navigational errors and the other because they were simply done. The race was proving more debilitating than even we had expected.

The meeting with the British Centrepoint team was to have a profound impact on our race in due course, but for now we had to get our heads around the notion that we had another 380 kilometres or so of ice and snow ahead. We hadn't considered the dramatic effect the 24-hour stop would have on us. Restarting our race at a time when we would have been settling in for the night previously, we realised that our routine, the only thing we could attempt to control, had been completely thrown out of sync by the 12-hour cycle shift. For the first half of the race, the sun had been positioned off our right shoulders at the start of the day, and as we progressed it would move behind us and end up off our left. Now we were trekking at "night", with the sun starting out at our left shoulders then circling in front of us before ending up off our right. There was no real difference in this process, but it played havoc with our heads, and we took a few days to get back in to some kind of reasonable routine. Once again we were presented with an example illustrating how important your mindset is in times of extended pressure and exertion.

As we neared the South Pole the temperature steadily dropped while, conversely, the terrain became steadily steeper. We would sometimes trek uphill for four hours at a time – so much for the "Don't worry, the plateau is flat" advice we had received – yet our spirits were strong. The commitment that Braam and I had made to each other before the race was critical to our success and our strategy to look after each other rather than ourselves was paying off, as it had for Bill and me on the Atlantic. To top it off, we had now joined forces with the Centrepoint men and our union had boosted our morale further.

Then, out of the blue, we had a bombshell dropped on us. During a call with the race organisers one week before the scheduled end of the race, we were informed that the cutoff date was being brought forward by two days. There was a huge weather system moving in and the last plane out from the Pole would have to leave before the storm hit. We had always been aware that the success or failure of our Antarctic venture would depend on the weather, as it had for Amundsen and Scott, and this was a potentially devastating blow. We were 210 kilometres from the finish line and would now be cutting things as fine as they could be. If we couldn't keep to the new deadline, the race organisers would send out a snow truck to collect us, we would not reach the Pole on foot and we would be disqualified.

It's easy to be demotivated at -45°C while suffering from frostbite, physical and mental exhaustion and massive weight loss. It would have been understandable to give up at this point – even responsible, as I had argued to myself in the mid-Atlantic two years previously – but we hadn't come this far to call it off when the prize was in sight. We adjusted our strategy to ensure the required distances were achieved every day, no matter what, and we powered on. Rather than breaking us, the news had empowered us with added motivation to push harder.

The final day of trekking to the Pole was very emotional. During our last 15-minute break between shifts, with the American research base, the Amundsen-Scott South Pole Station, in sight, Braam and I toasted the Centrepoint team with a dinky bottle of Johnnie Walker. And then we stood up and turned to each other and said, for the last time, "Well… Shall we?"

After 24 days of racing, we reached the South Pole with 90 minutes to spare before the official cut off. On our arrival the air temperature was -48°C.

We cried with joy in the last kilometres, not just because we were finishing what was easily one of the toughest endurance races in the world, but because we had done so despite such great odds. We had had the least polar experience of all seven teams to start, and yet we were one of only three to officially finish. The Norwegians had comfortably won the race, with a strong British (actually Welsh) team in second, but this was the proudest third place of my life. Braam and I had connected as friends and comrades. We had shared our pains and laughed at each other's jokes – Braam's hilarious, mine terrible. We had done it together and by the end of it we knew everything about each other's lives. It's not often in life that we get the opportunity to bond so closely with a fellow human, and without our grand race Braam and I would surely not be the best of friends we are today. We will forever be bonded as brothers in arms, kindred spirits who have walked in the footsteps of the legends of polar exploration. The story and dream were complete, and once again we had come full circle with success and significance.

Since returning from Antarctica, I have often been asked how we did it when other, supposedly better-prepared, teams failed. I believe we were able to conquer our Eighth Summit, using all the experience we had accumulated in our careers and many of the lessons gathered here in this book.

Exhausted to the core, but with great pride, we raised the South African flag over the Ceremonial South Pole mirror ball (which is situated a short distance from the actual Geographic South Pole). Then we struck the seals on the SA Mint Company's Centenary coins at the South Pole – a world first. Our mission was over. Unlike Scott, though, we didn't have to trek home.

WELL, SHALL WE?
Humour as a survival strategy

"Against the assault of laughter nothing can stand."
– Mark Twain

One of my favourite movies is Ridley Scott's modern war classic *Black Hawk Down*, starring Eric Bana and Josh Hartnett. Based on the book of the same name, the film recounts the events of the Battle of Mogadishu, fought between United States forces and Somali militia men over the afternoon, evening and morning of 3 and 4 October 1993.

Having been deployed to Somalia in 1992 as part of a greater United Nations peacekeeping force during a time of severe famine and civil war, US forces were later tasked with the capture of the warlord and self-proclaimed president-to-be Mohamed Farrah Aidid. Operation Gothic Serpent, as it was code-named, was executed almost exclusively by special-operations units: US Army Rangers, "Delta Force" operators and Navy SEALs, supported by a specialised helicopter squadron known as the Night Stalkers. These guys were the elite of the elite, serious professionals, and when they set out on 3 October to snatch two of Aidid's lieutenants from a downtown Mogadishu hotel, they would not have imagined the disaster to come. Though it involved less than 24 hours of suburban fighting, the Battle of Mogadishu, known in Somalia as the Day of the Rangers, would become the bloodiest day in US warfare since the Vietnam War, with 18 soldiers killed and scores wounded. Somali casualties were impossible to verify but may well have numbered in the thousands.

The assault began as planned, with Delta Force soldiers being choppered into the city and seizing their targets, but when a young Ranger slipped from a helicopter and had to be evacuated, things quickly fell apart. Somali fighters shot down two supporting Black Hawk helicopters in quick succession with rocket-propelled grenades, and what should have been a simple half-hour mission turned into a vicious overnight standoff in the city.

In the movie, the action ebbs and flows, with intense and graphic firefights being followed by periods of uneasy quiet. Eventually, once night falls, the US forces find themselves holed up in a collection of shot-up buildings. There is no fighting, but also no escape while the wounded are tended and an evacuation plan put in place. In one room the Rangers can only watch as one of their comrades bleeds slowly to death; it's an agonising scene that leads to what is perhaps the moral climax of the movie. In this period of stressful waiting, Delta operator Hoot (played by Bana) and Ranger Matt Eversmann (Hartnett) share a profound exchange about life, choices and the way we cope with things. There is a superb moment when the first rays of the sun show over the rooftops and we know the battle must start up again in earnest. Hoot turns to Eversmann and says in a calm voice with just the hint of a smile, "Well, shall we?"

The way he says it, they may as well be popping out for a coffee together or perhaps a nice picnic in a meadow somewhere, rather than heading back into a bloody and brutal battle. As you may have realised, it's a sense of irony that I appreciate – a moment of humour in a decidedly non-comedic movie.

Right from the start of the race *"Well, shall we?"* became the tongue-in-cheek Antarctic war cry for Braam and me. We weren't heading out into pitched battle in the streets of Mogadishu, but we were certainly venturing into dangerous and brutal conditions.

One of the methods I use to stay positive on my expeditions, as mentioned previously, is to incorporate a routine that is enforced under almost all conditions. It allows your daily activities to become second nature and it helps to banish negative thoughts – and if you can incorporate a little humour into it, all the better. During the first Atlantic row with Bill, we hit upon the "90 minutes closer to Antigua!" mantra. Now, with Braam, it was "Well, shall we?"

At the start of each day we would finish our morning routine in the safety and warmth of the tent, systematically going about our business as the freezing and inhospitable Antarctic waited patiently for us beyond the tent flap. My duty was to get the cooking system up and running while Braam used the time to sort out the dressings on his feet. I would get the stoves going, always a tedious task, then melt ice for water for the day and make porridge. When we were kitted up and ready to head outside into the cold, we would pack the sledges and take down the tent as quickly as possible. This last manoeuvre in particular, with the two of us on our knees dismantling and rolling, shoulder to shoulder, was one that took practised teamwork so that we could get it done without developing frostnip or the early stages of hypothermia. Hanging around in -30°C temperatures or worse is no joke unless you're dressed in proper cold-weather clothing – which we weren't at this point. Rather, we would be in our trekking gear, which is perfect for hauling a pulk through ice and snow while burning calories and generating plenty of body heat, but not for standing around in said ice and snow. Just a few minutes of relative inactivity could be enough to do us damage, an early morning reminder of the constant challenges we faced in Antarctica.

Once the tent was packed away on my sledge and we were ready to trek, we would shoot off a short prayer and then look at each other. One of us would say, "Well?" – and the other would reply, "Shall we?"

Later, at the end of our two daily 15-minute breaks we would do exactly the same.

"Well, shall we?"

Yes, we shall.

How and why could such a repetitive and even silly-sounding routine have any great effect on us, two grown men undertaking a serious physical expedition? It boils down to the concept that underscores every adventure I take and that resurfaces again and again throughout these pages: having a positive attitude towards whatever it is you are doing. Because one of the keys to a positive mindset is the ability to have fun and laugh.

One of the earlier pre-race discussions I had with Braam was about the importance of consistently focusing on having fun and finding the humour in our situation. In a high-stress environment, laughter is even more important than usual. One of the major challenges an individual faces when taking on long and dangerous expeditions is the inevitable exposure to prolonged periods of stress. When you're constantly stressed your immune system takes strain, which can open you up to all sorts of physical problems. You don't have to row an ocean or trek to the South Pole to be familiar with this notion; any stressful spell at work or an extended period of family problems can manifest physically as headaches, back pain, body twitches and the like, or in full-blown sickness, whether it's irritable bowel syndrome, German measles or plain old flu. It's the way of the fast-paced, competitive modern world.

Putting yourself in a stressful situation triggers your natural fight-or-flight responses. In order to cope with a possible threat or difficult situation, the body secretes adrenaline and other hormones. These increase heart rate, blood pressure and oxygen intake, and temporarily shut down the immune system and other functions that are not immediately necessary during an emergency. This makes you less sensitive to pain and more able to focus intensely on fighting or fleeing, and is just what you need when you're confronted by a pack of hyenas on the African savannah, or even when you're writing an important exam and need complete focus. But repeated exposure to stressful situations can be damaging in the long term. Whether we're sitting in front of a computer every day crunching numbers or pulling a 90-kilogram sledge through snow and ice, we need strategies for minimising and managing the impact of ongoing stresses on our bodies. This is where laughter is so crucial because, as clichéd as it may sound, a simple smile can turn a bad day into a good day.

Laughter literally is medicine. When you laugh your body undergoes physical changes, just as it does when you're stressed. First off, it causes you to take in more oxygen, which means muscles and essential organs are able to perform better. It also triggers the release of endorphins, the same feel-good hormones produced during exercise and sex and when you eat chocolate. They restrain negative emotions, while increasing motivation, mood and sense of wellbeing. Your confidence levels are given a boost and a brief sense of satisfaction is achieved. Not only does laughing make you feel good, it also lowers your blood pressure, improves breathing, regulates your heartbeat and boosts your immune system. As a result your stress levels immediately begin to drop. The physical act of laughing and smiling even acts as an analgesic, improving your tolerance for pain – and Braam and I were going to need all the help we could get in that department.

The two of us made an agreement to try to swap at least one joke every day – even on the days that we were feeling our worst, which were of course the days we needed a laugh the most. Luckily for me, Braam has a brilliant sense of humour, which comes with a whole quiver of jokes that I am amazed he can even begin to remember. He would ski up next to me when the ice conditions allowed it, and say, "Hey Pete, have I ever told you the joke about the farmer and his bulls?" No he hadn't, and I was delighted to hear it!

I, on the other hand, simply cannot remember jokes. I have an entirely underwhelming collection of about three jokes in my memory banks. Sadly, I had already tried them out on Braam long before the race began, so Kim came up with a good idea: she found me a joke book to take to Antarctica, containing a range of funny stories and one-liners, from the hilarious to the truly lame. She even went through the book and highlighted the better ones. Mindful of our hauling considerations, she ensured the book was a light softcover, but even a hardcover would have been worth its weight in gold.

At some point, often during one of the two short breaks we allowed ourselves between trekking sessions, I would pull out the book from my jacket and rattle off a joke. Often the more pathetic it was, the funnier it seemed and the more it seemed to cheer us up. The silliness took our minds off the conditions around us and bonded us even more as a team.

And that is actually a funny thing (if you'll excuse the pun). Because here's the trump card: smiling works even when you're faking it. You can trick your body into releasing all those feelgood hormones even when the smile on your face isn't a "genuine" one. You may feel like a bit of con if you think about it too hard, but if you just plant a cheesy grin on your face and keep it there for a while, it will start boosting your sense of wellbeing.

This phenomenon was apparent in the blog reports from Mick Birchall, the Atlantic pairs rower who had to find a partner for the 2010 crossing at the last minute and ended up with the rather different Lia Ditton, not an ideal scenario before such a demanding expedition. Unsurprisingly, their race was a somewhat fractious one, especially early on. Following advice from Cliffy, Mick reported as follows.

The remaining 1,692 miles looms like an impossibly large number, but our spirits are high, our manners have improved and we've been practising being kind to each other! One suggestion we received was from the Van Kets camp. Last race Pete and Bill Godfrey won the pairs class and at oar changeover they made a pact to exchange several positive words. One example given was, "Hey Bill! I got you 90 minutes closer to Antigua" – and Bill had to respond with something grateful and positive like, "Yee Ha!" or "Thanks Pete!" So we've started saying something along those lines and apart from being mildly comical in that American drive-thru "Now, you have yourself a nice day!" superficial way, I like it and I think it will help.

The bottom line is this: when you laugh or smile, not only do you feel good, your mental and physical health improves, too. Don't be afraid to crack lame jokes! It's for a good cause: your health.

> *Lame Antarctic joke, example 1:*
> Late one night a nun is standing on a street outside Sandton City. A fairly inebriated man staggers past, slows down, turns and walks back to her.
> "Sister, I hope I don't offend, but I am Catholic and I've always fantasised about kissing a nun."
> "No offence taken. I've fantasised about kissing a gorgeous young man. What do you say we slip into the alley and indulge in our wildest dreams? No-one ever need know."
> In the dark the nun kisses the man with passion. Back on the street the man smiles, waves a goodbye kiss and says, " Oh sister, a quick confession. I'm not Catholic."
> "That's okay, my son, I'm not a nun. My name is Kevin and I've just come from a fancy-dress party."

Having done her fair share of multi-day endurance events herself, Kim was very aware of this phenomenon and my belief in it. As a result, she came up with another clever plan, to try to put a smile on my face every morning even while she was thousands of kilometres away.

Part of my morning routine involved relocating a daily snack pack from my pulk to my waist belt. The snack packs included the provisions Braam and I needed for our two daily breaks. Typically they would include a variety of treats such as Sugus sweets (my favourite), a small packet of chips and wine gums, and Kim and Hannah had kindly taken it upon themselves to put them together for me in Cape Town before we left. Unbeknown to me, they had also included a note in each pack to serve as encouragement for that day. It was a brilliant idea. As soon as I worked out that Kim had included one in each pack, I looked forward to opening them every morning. Seeing what treats I had in store was great, but it was the note that I anticipated with huge delight and which lifted me despite the pain and suffering that lay in wait that day. I would rip my pack open, read the note and then read it again aloud for Braam. Here's an example of one such note.

Today is a new day. Begin it well. Put yesterday behind you. Suffer the pain of discipline today or suffer the pain of regret forever. Better sore than sorry. I don't have to tell you any of this because you know it. Love you and praying for you all the time, my Glove. We love you madly. Xxxx Hannah and Me xxxx

---

Kim knows me so well. ("Glove" is her nickname for me, by the way.) She knew that saying something like this would really psych me up in entirely the right way. Being able to begin each day with a big smile on my face sent all the right messages to my body and was perfect for my mindset.

The great polar explorers who came to fame at the turn of the 20th century were hardy, gritty men, an extraordinary percentage of whom died while on the job. As examples, Robert Scott famously perished while trekking back from the South Pole in 1912; Ernest Shackleton had a heart attack on the island of South George in 1922; and Roald Amundsen went down in a flying boat somewhere in the Arctic Ocean in 1928. Titans of a far more serious age, these men weren't exactly jesters.

Yet, if you read Amundsen's diary entries from his great expeditions, there is a sense of cheerfulness missing that you won't find in Scott's. Amundsen wasn't just the first to reach the South Pole; he was an explorer of great renown around the world

186

and a national treasure in Norway, leading the first navigation of the famed Northwest Passage between 1903 and 1906, and the first undisputed journey to the North Pole in 1925. When I read his diaries I always get a sense that he is focusing on the positives around him.

This is an extract from his diary, translated from Norwegian, written on 12 December 1911, a couple of days before his team of five men reached the South Pole.

Our best day up here. It has been calm for most of the day – with burning sunshine. The going and terrain have been the same.

Luckily the snow crust is so hard that sledges and doggies sink in very little. The hypsometer still shows us descending, albeit very gently, so that it must be assumed that we have not only established the highest point of the plateau, but also are sinking down towards the other side. We have done 15 nautical miles today, and according to the midday obs. are now at 89°30'30". Obs. and dead reckoning agree brilliantly every day. We can only trust one of our sextants – the Fram sextant – the other one has unfortunately suffered a blow and proved not to be reliable. HH W. & I now share the Fram sextant.

[A hypsometer was a device used for estimating altitude by calibrating the temperature at which water boils. Sextants were used to measure the altitude of the sun, or any heavenly body, when calculating an observer's latitude.]

This is in contrast to Scott's diary entry from the same day.

Camp 34. We have had a hard day, and during the forenoon it was my team which made the heaviest weather of the work. We got bogged again and again, and, do what we would, the sledge dragged like lead. The others were working hard but nothing to be compared to us. At 2.30 I halted for lunch, pretty well cooked, and there was disclosed the secret of our trouble in a thin film with some hard knots of ice on the runners. Evans' team had been sent off in advance, and we didn't – couldn't! – catch them, but they saw us camp and break camp and followed suit. I really dreaded starting after lunch, but after some trouble to break the sledge out, we went ahead without a hitch, and in a mile or two recovered our leading place with obvious ability to keep it. At 6 I saw the other teams were flagging and so camped at 7, meaning to turn out earlier to-morrow and start a better routine. We have done about 8 or perhaps 9 miles (stat.) – the sledge-meters are hopeless on such a surface.

[continued]

From his diary transcripts, it seems to me that Amundsen had a more positive attitude to his expedition and his team, and that this upbeat, slightly cheeky approach was always more likely to lead to success.

Scott, on the other hand, seemed to have a gloomier air about him. On one occasion he wrote, "The scene about us is the same as we have seen for many a day, and shall see for many a day to come – a scene so wildly and awfully desolate that it cannot fail to impress one with gloomy thoughts." It may sound harsh to judge him in this way – bearing in mind he achieved great things and was encountering literally the worst conditions on earth – but I believe that this may well have been one of the contributing factors to the demise of the British expedition.

During the initial acclimatisation trek of the South Pole Centenary Race, the teams all struggled while ascending the steep glaciers up to the Antarctic plateau. There was a lot of complaining, with many competitors focusing on the negative things going on around us. I have no doubt that this set the tone for the teams who later pulled out of the race.

As ever, it all comes down mental attitude. Fun and laughter point to a positive state of mind. Grumbling and complaining reflect negative thinking. The former is a recipe for success, while the latter will soon see you slipping into an uncontrollable spiral of self-destruction.

> *Lame Antarctic joke, example 2:*
> A blonde, wanting to earn some money as a handyman, started canvassing a wealthy neighbourhood. At the first house she asked the owner if he had any jobs for her to do.
> "What will you charge to paint my porch?" he asked.
> "R300," she replied
> The man agreed and told her that everything she needed for the job would be in the garage. A short time later, the blonde came to the door to collect her money.
> "Finished already?" the man asked.
> "Yes," the blonde replied "and I had paint left over so I gave it two coats. By the way – its not a Porsche; it's a Ferrari."

Still, sometimes you have to be careful you don't laugh too hard – especially at -45°C. On one occasion, about two weeks into the race, Braam told me a joke (now forgotten, of course) while we were taking one of our daily breaks. It was so funny that I was soon crying with laughter, and as I cried the tears were freezing on my cheeks. Not a good thing. I quickly put on my goggles, stood up and said, "Well?"

Braam answered, "Shall we?!" – and off we trekked, buoyed by laughter.

TEAM CENTREPOINT
Understanding the benefit of helping others succeed

*"Give the world the best you have,
and the best will come back to you."*
– Mother Teresa

The words of Mother Teresa above are a universal law that we are all aware of, in a theoretical sense at least. Put your best into something and you will get the best out of it; this is straightforward enough. But sometimes you need a real physical event to understand the notion that when you do your best *for someone else* you will be the one who benefits just as much, or even more. I have experienced elements of this truth many times in my life, but the Centenary Race to the South Pole produced the most telling example I know. The greatest life lesson I took from our race across Antarctica began at about the halfway mark.

Six days into the race, on 8 January, Braam skied up to me shortly after our first 15-minute break of the day. "Hey Pete," he said, "I don't know if I'm going mad, but can you see those specks off to our left? I think it could be another team."
The great white plains of Antarctica can play tricks on your senses, and I strained my eyes in the direction he was pointing. There was some ice build-up inside my goggles so I had to take them off. Eventually I could make out what Braam had seen

several kilometres away. It was hard to pick out much detail, but it was definitely another team and it seemed to be moving at about the same speed we were.

"Any idea who they could be?" I asked.

We didn't know how any of our fellow competitors were faring at this stage. The most we could deduce about the far-off specks was that they couldn't be the Norwegians; they would be days ahead of us by now. After a spell of squinting into the distance, we could make out three figures, which gave us another clue. Braam guessed it was Centrepoint, one of the British teams. If he was right that would be fantastic news, as it meant we were keeping in touch with one of the more fancied teams.

We kept an eye on them as we progressed along the undulating terrain, watching them disappear into ice valleys and then reappear a few hours later – and so it went for the next couple of days, watching them come and go on the horizon.

By this stage the epic challenge of the race had revealed itself. Everything about what we were doing was difficult, from the obvious to the less obvious. The intense physical output required to haul our pulks was anticipated (though anticipation didn't make it easier!). The frustrating difficulty of performing basic tasks such as blowing your nose, scratching an itch on your face, keeping your goggles clear, clicking into your skis or going to the loo were less expected. The inability to sleep properly, despite near-total exhaustion, was a particularly debilitating problem.

On Day 8 we woke to a shrieking wind. "Woke" implies we had slept beforehand, but the fitful rest we were getting hardly qualifies. The whistling wind and our constantly flapping tent, combined with our regular coughing and the never-ending sunshine, prevented us from getting the deep sleep we so desperately needed. Braam's chest remained a concern, and by now I too had developed the high-altitude hack familiar to mountaineers around the world. Caused by overexertion while breathing in cold, dry air, it is a form of bronchitis that in worst-case scenarios can cause coughing fits that pull chest muscles or break ribs. On Mount Everest it is known as the Khumbu cough.

I sat up in my sleeping bag and wormed my way to the inner zip of the tent, which was the portal to the separate cooking area. It was cold – really cold. The cooking area had a smoky look, as if it had been sprayed with a fine layer of liquid oxygen. As I leaned over to unzip the outer flysheet to get a look at the conditions outside, sheets of thin ice fell from the ceiling onto my sleeping bag and down the back of my neck, making me wince with cold. I put on my sunglasses – looking out over the bright ice without them will lead to eye burn in no time – and as I unzipped the tent a feeling of dread overwhelmed me. The weather conditions were particularly dangerous, with frighteningly low temperatures exacerbated by a nasty wind. I sensed that if we went out there we would be putting our lives on the line; there were a lot of good reasons to stay exactly where we were until conditions improved. Braam's health was my main concern, and if this hadn't been a race the decision would have been easy. No-go.

But we had to go.

I zipped the tent closed, sat back, lit the stoves and started the morning water-and-food routine. I knew the daily routine would sort out my head. This was a race and we had to progress relentlessly unless we wanted to jeopardise the dream of making it to the pole ahead of our cutoff time. Despite our reservations, we slowly kicked into gear and managed to get going.

We soon spotted the team that had been ghosting in the distance ahead of us for two days – except that instead of three figures we could see only two. Had they lost a man or was this another team altogether? Perhaps the two-man Welsh team? Or were the conditions producing an illusion of two when perhaps there were three? It was a mystery that provided us with a great distraction and lots to speculate about in the coming days, but no certainty. The enigmatic two-man team would remain in our sights until the compulsory 24-hour stop at the halfway mark.

By Day 10 of the race, Braam's condition had dramatically

improved and he was beginning to get a bit more sleep – and so was I. This was a huge breakthrough and a reason to be happy. It was also my father's 80th birthday, another reason to celebrate. It is one of the disappointments of my adventuring career that I end up missing so many Christmases, New Year's parties, birthdays and other occasions. I was really sad to be missing my dad's great milestone and I pictured my whole family getting together without me. I did, however, manage to call home on the satellite phone. My father seemed very tearful as we spoke, but with the bad line and the noise of the wind I was unsure whether this was because he didn't like being 80 or because he was worried about me. I would have to make up for missing his big day on my return.

A further reason for celebration was the fact that it was a brilliant day – a warm and pleasant -15°C. Virtually tropical.

During the first shift of the day we experienced a few hours of complete whiteout, a quite surreal experience when the light is diffused in such an even way across the pale landscape that you can't make out the horizon and so cannot differentiate between the ice beneath you and the sky above you. No shadows are cast and no surface irregularities are visible, which means that beyond the end of your skis your depth perception is shot. It's very disorientating, like being trapped inside a giant white marshmallow, and you have to rely on your GPS and compass to ensure you're travelling in the right direction. (The compass isn't accurate so near the pole, but it works perfectly for maintaining a heading.)

As we travelled along in these strange conditions, we became aware of ruts in the ice that looked like the tracks of a vehicle. Was this a sign of recent human activity? A little further on we made out a dark object ahead of us, but it was only when we were nearly on top of it that we could see it was a large tyre. It looked like the type of tyre used on the race organisers' Arctic Trucks. Originally developed in Iceland, these are usually Toyota bakkies that have been completely overhauled for serious ice and snow conditions and are easily identified by their enormous tyres. (*Top Gear* fans will recognise them from the expedition to the Magnetic North Pole.) We stopped for a long while to consider our find and to discuss its reason for being there. It was wonderful to see and talk about something new and different, the first foreign object we had seen in a long time – a noteworthy topic of conversation indeed!

We set off again, this time skiing in the tyre tracks, which were harder than the surrounding ice and snow and thus easier to move across. What luck.

A few minutes later I was sure I could hear the sound of a distant engine, but with conditions playing the usual tricks on my senses I couldn't be sure. I said nothing and put it down to a possible supply plane flying to the American-run research station at the South Pole. Then I heard it again.

"Hey Braam, did you hear that?"

"No?" he replied, unsure. We stopped and removed our fur-lined hoods.

There it was again. The throbbing sound of an engine.

We looked up to see if it was a plane, but we could make out nothing in the whiteout. Moments later the noise was getting louder and closer and our eyes nearly popped out of our heads when we finally saw the cause of it: a large twin-cab Arctic Truck emerging from the white haze on its oversized tyres. It was one of the competition trucks and it was heading straight for us. The vehicle stopped and two familiar figures emerged: the race doctor, Ian Davies, and an Icelandic engineer called Gísli Jónsson. People! Combined with a tyre and a vehicle all in one morning, this was almost too much stimulation for us to handle!

The four of us chatted for a few minutes, and Ian confirmed that we were now very close to the halfway mark. While we were talking I noticed another person huddled in the back of the vehicle; it was strange that he hadn't come out too. When Gísli opened the door to get back in, I got a good look and saw that it was Andrew Carnie, one of the Centrepoint team members.

After our somewhat bizarre meeting, Braam and I chatted for

several hours about what could have happened to Andrew. We could only conclude that he must be ill or injured and had been rescued as a result. That would account for the three-man team that had inexplicably become a two-man team.

It was all very intriguing. We hoped to find out all the details at our next stop.

The halfway point was nothing more than a couple of tents at a GPS coordinate, but we were excited by the milestone and the thought of interacting with more people. It helped, too, that the weather had settled and wind dropped. From about four kilometres out we could make out Centrepoint's familiar tent; its presence meant they were less than a day ahead of us. There were no signs of any other competitors.

On our arrival we were greeted again by Ian and Gísli. There was little time for socialising and we quickly set up our tent and disappeared inside to maximise the benefit of our 24-hour stop. We would use this time to rest and to repair and sort out gear. For one, I had to sew up my inner gloves, which were coming apart at the seams at the end of the fingertips.

Ian visited us for a brief check up and confirmed that we were fit to continue. During his visit he told us that they had indeed picked up Andrew a couple of days previously after he had fallen and broken his arm. His teammates, Ben Boyne and Jason Bolton, had continued on without him and arrived six hours ahead of us. Ian also brought us up to date with news of the other teams. The Norwegians were coming first, the Welsh were in second and, now that Centrepoint had been disqualified due to the assistance given to Andrew, we were miraculously in third. The other three teams had all quit.

Despite his broken arm, Andrew was determined to rejoin Ben and Jason and ski to the finish together. He had managed to convince Ian that he would be okay as long as he had some good painkillers and buy-in from his teammates. The race organisers reluctantly agreed after explaining exactly what the risks were and getting him to sign a wad of indemnities and waivers. Though they were officially out of the race, it gave Centrepoint the opportunity of reaching the pole together.

Eighteen hours later the British team were set to head out on the second leg. We heard them packing their pulks and reluctantly wriggled out of our warm sleeping bags to give them a good send off. As they disappeared into the distance Ian turned to me.

"Pete, that team is never going to make it to the South Pole," he said.

"What do you mean?" I asked.

"Well, Andrew is going to really have a hard time of it pulling his sledge and James and Ben are not in a condition to carry his load."

There was a silence for a while and then he glanced at me and said, "If they had some help it may be possible. Just throwing it out there."

Braam and I returned to our sleeping bags for a few more hours' respite before we were due to head off after Andrew, Ben and Jason into the white wilderness. The British team dominated our conversation. Just as Braam and I had done, they had spent a huge amount of time, energy and resources putting their expedition together. They were also passionate about raising funds for charity. Where we were doing it for Operation Smile, they were doing it for Centerpoint, a well-known organisation in the UK that assists young homeless people. They had a dream to make it to the South Pole and that dream was in jeopardy. As things stood, the story they would have to tell their grandchildren one day was probably not going to have a happy ending. We had the opportunity to change that and to keep the story alive.

In the end we felt we had no choice but to offer them whatever help we could, despite the real chance that it could jeopardise our own race. It would mean splitting Andrew's kit between the two of us, but we believed we could handle the extra load. Andrew would still have to ski with his pulk and some basic survival equipment, but it would greatly reduce his physical challenge.

We weren't at all sure that Andrew would accept our assistance – adventurers are sometimes known to have oversized egos! – but we had decided to offer it, on condition that Centrepoint agreed to adopt our skiing regime and routine.

Decision made, it was time to strike out once more, the last push to the pole. The 24-hour rest period had been a welcome break but it had flown by in a blink. With a mixture of excitement and dread, we headed off following the British tracks.

It didn't take us long to catch up. We saw the Centrepoint tent from a distance, but there was no steam rising from it which suggested the cookers were off and they were resting. When we drew alongside we called out to them to let them know that if they wanted assistance we were prepared to help. If they agreed to take us up on it, we could meet at our next rest stop, redistribute the kit and continue together according to our schedule. We were unable to stop for too long because of the cold and continued on our way, leaving them to consider their options.

We were sleeping in our tent when Andrew, Ben and Jason skied silently past and posted a letter into our cooking area. I found it when I woke and began the cooking process. "Had a tough one yesterday and think we'll need to take up your kind offer very soon if that's OK," it read, before suggesting we discuss details when next we reached their tent.

The following day we caught up with them once again and instituted our new plan, relocating most of Andrew's gear onto our pulks and setting off together. Team Mission Possible had joined up with team Centrepoint. The two of us had become five.

This was the beginning of a brilliant time for all of us, and although the additional weight on our pulks took a toll, the company more than made up for it. Andrew, Ben and Jason were great young guys with an admirable ambition to raise heaps of money for their chosen charity. In fact, they were aiming to raise £1 million by 2015 from a number of events, and wanted to finish off by rowing the Atlantic together – so I had some good advice to give them.

Jason later told us that had we not offered our help to them that first day after the halfway point, they would have pulled out of the race. They were stretched to breaking point and Andrew's injury was just too much to handle.

As the days passed and we trekked on together, it dawned on me that the assistance and support from our team to theirs was actually a two-way street. Everyone was well aware that we were helping them, but we were less aware that they were helping us. They were of no physical assistance – in fact, they were the opposite; a physical hindrance – but they were certainly assisting with what was happening inside our heads.

I am reluctant to compare Andrew, Ben and Jason to animals, but indulge me for a moment. On my solo row across the Atlantic I had my six dorados who lived with me for six weeks, becoming the extra heartbeats that motivated me from under my boat. They connected with me and they kept me entertained. They would have been of no physical assistance to me during an emergency, but they provided me with a great sense of security. They were good for my head. It was exactly the same with the Centrepoint team. Having them around was good for our heads. Their goal was now our goal; we were doubly motivated. Though we had been worried about the extra exertion required to pull Andrew's equipment, our decision actually worked in our favour. The good that we had done in offering to help our British competitors was coming back to us now and paying huge dividends. What should have been the most painful part of the expedition, the final agonising push to the end, became the most enjoyable part. Even when our deadline was moved forward two days due to incoming weather, we came together as an enhanced team, more motivated and more upbeat, and we accepted the new deadline as a challenge to rise to. In the end, the ten days we spent trekking with Andrew, Ben and Jason was the highlight of our polar expedition.

Braam: Pete and I would never have been able to help the Brits to the Pole if we weren't solid together. It was our joint strength they picked up on and they wouldn't have accepted our offer if they hadn't recognised that. It wasn't about winning; it was about friendship. It wasn't about our country beating their country; it was about unity. We are brothers through extreme adversity. Friends for life. What a privilege!

As Jan Smuts once said (specfically of the Allies' decision to support Greece after it was invaded by the Nazis during World War II), "To do the right thing is generally the right thing to do."

We often ignore cries for help or turn a blind eye to people who are struggling because we believe we are already too far stretched. Where, we ask ourselves, will we find the time and resources and energy to help others when we're barely getting by ourselves? Sometimes we intentionally avoid helping others – be it competitors or colleagues – because we believe that their failure will aid our success. The lesson I learnt in Antarctica is that the opposite is true. There is no measuring the personal benefit of helping another person to succeed. You will always reap what you sow tenfold.

BEHIND THE SCENES
Surrounding yourself with the best team possible

"If you want to go fast then go alone.
If you want to go far then go together."
– African saying, unknown origin

Whether you're starting a business or trekking to the South Pole, surrounding yourself with the best possible team of people is one of the most important factors to consider for achieving success. Once I have the dream or vision for a particular venture, my second step is to seek out the right people to take along for the ride.

This has been a critical factor in all my major expeditions and, if ever I had doubted its significance, the support of those involved in my solo Atlantic crossing in 2010 drove it home. Each of them – Kim and Hannah (obviously!); Cliffy and his wife Tracey; Tjaart, my weatherman; Uwe Jaspersen, the builder of *Nyamezela*; Steven du Toit, who fitted her out; Robert Galley, my electrician; my engineering friends Niels Andersen and Arno van de Merwe; my personal trainer Caron Williams; Julian Dallamore, my liaison at Liberty; and others – played a vital role in getting me across the Atlantic. If just one of them had underperformed, the entire expedition would have been put in jeopardy, and it was because of this team effort that we decided to call the documentary of the trip *Not Alone*.

Similarly, Braam and I needed a champion team to steer us to the South Pole, but putting it together involved two considerations I hadn't had to worry about on the solo row. First, we were both out of our element. I knew the ocean (as much as one can); I didn't know snow and ice and impossibly cold Antarctic conditions. Neither did Braam; he was an expert in endurance running (among other things). We would have to rely on people more knowledgeable than us to help us to achieve our goal.

Second, Braam and I would form a team within a team, and the way we interacted would be critical to the success of the venture. If we didn't work well together we didn't stand a chance.

The obvious conundrum arose in the early stages of our preparation: how do we form a support team to assist us with all aspects of the expedition when we don't know anyone who is truly familiar with Antarctic conditions? You've got to start somewhere, and in such instances the best tactic is often to rely on that good friend Google. We realised we would have to spend a great deal of time researching information for ourselves, so that's exactly what we did.

Then, to our amazement – though these things seem to happen more often than you'd think possible – we discovered that an experienced polar guide had recently moved to Cape Town. Andrew Thompson wasn't just any guide; he worked for the race organisers, Extreme World Races, so Braam and I jumped at the opportunity to consult with him as soon as it arose. In the following months Andrew shared an incredible amount of hard-earned cold-weather knowledge with us, and we were delighted to have him on our side. We were very grateful for his involvement by the end of the trip, and if there is a lesson here it's possibly to recognise an important resource or opportunity when one falls into your lap, and then maximise it. (Andrew did, however, get one thing wrong. He told us that once up on the high plateau at 3,200 metres the terrain is flat all the way to the pole. This was not the case; it was everything but flat!)

Meanwhile, Kim and Hedda, our respective partners, once again became the mainstay of our team. The emotional and logistical support they offered during the hectic three months before the race was paramount. We simply couldn't have done it without them. During the race their continued support was vital and we would call them daily for much-needed, energising contact. Of course, they ran our respective households while we were gone, as well as all the never-ending race admin – and I know how tough that can all be.

Kim's blog: When Peter is away, I need to deal with the inconvenience of being a single parent. (I have great respect for people who do this all the time.) It can get pretty hectic trying to earn a living, look after a small child, do all the housework (Patricia, my domestic, is uncannily on extended annual or maternity leave every time Peter is away), run the home admin and finances, do the DIY, fix the car (hooter, air-con, tyres, lights all inexplicably give up the ghost during expeditions!), evict snakes and bats from my home, operate as Pete's PRO, churn out information for the websites, book flights and accommodation without ETAs, apply for visas and train for my own expeditions/races all while offering Peter emotional support 24/7...

This sort of scenario is quite common during expeditions: I have a work-related but ignored deadline. I am on the phone conducting an interview with a newspaper which is unable to reach Peter, the gardener electrocutes himself with the lawn mower and the neighbour's dog decides to maul him in his weakened state, Hannah bellows from the bathroom that the toilet roll has run out, someone arrives in the driveway and begins hooting as the washing machine inexplicably begins to overflow all over the floor...

Besides the technical and emotional support we needed in preparation for the challenge, the third key element of this particular venture was the involvement of our filmmakers during the race itself. Danie Ferreira of Urban Brew Studios was an obvious candidate for us to approach, an old friend and an expert in his field. I knew he would love the challenge and excitement of filming in Antarctica and I trusted his judgment completely. When he brought in the father-and-son duo of Paul and Henri van Schalkwyk, along with Stafford Robinson, I simply assumed they would all be superb filmmakers. They were, and they were good people, too – important under stressful conditions. I got on really well with all of them, and I especially enjoyed the company of Paul who was a gentle and peaceful character. Tragically, Paul died in March 2014 in a light-aircraft crash. Given the enduring bonds that form on expeditions of this nature, we were all terribly saddened by the news.

As brilliant as our support crew was, in the end Braam was the most important teammate on this particular trip. When deciding whether or not to enter the race, I had to consider two primary questions: first, whether I could do the thing; and second, whether I could live with Braam in Antarctica for 24 hours a day, seven days a week, for six weeks. We were going to be trekking through an extreme environment, eating and sleeping in the same space, suffering together, motivating each other and relying on each other in frequently hazardous conditions. Hardly a minute in six weeks would go by when we weren't within talking distance (even if the wind was so loud we couldn't hear what we were saying).

When people are taken from the comfort zones of their daily lives and placed for an extended time in a foreign and hostile environment – of which Antarctica is just about the perfect example – it is common for them to undergo substantial personality changes. I have observed this many times during the ocean crossings I have undertaken on yachts. It is interesting to see how many of the crew will become paranoid, oversensitive and self-absorbed only four or five days into a trip. Typically, they will start taking care of themselves only, to the detriment of others, refusing their fair share of duties and not helping out where they may have previously. Sometimes they will hoard communal supplies in their cabins. When conditions become tough or even dangerous, otherwise competent people can completely withdraw into themselves and become helplessly dependent. On winter in Antarctica, Ranulph Fiennes writes:

> "There are few groups of individuals who will live together for long periods in the cold and dark without dissension and tension rearing their ugly heads. Careful team selection processes can minimize trouble from individuals, and many polar authorities use tests already devised by selection boards for police, top executives, army officers and air crew. The most apt for would-be polar winter base applicants is that used to select submarine crews."

We may not have been wintering in Antarctica, but both Braam and I were well aware of what Fiennes describes, and neither of us would have considered entering the Centenary Race to the South Pole without having complete faith and trust in our partner. Happily, from the moment Braam called me to invite me to be his teammate for the race, I had complete peace of mind that he was the right person to be joining forces with and that we would operate well as a team. Just as I had when Bill asked me to row with him six years earlier, I knew that Braam was cut out for this type of thing. Before he'd even properly formulated the invitation, my answer was a resounding yes.

I had followed Braam's endurance-running career and met with him two years previously to discuss Kim's expedition. He had the ideal attitude towards extreme endurance events. His head was strong and in the right place, which he had proved with his epic runs along the Great Wall of China and the entire coast of South Africa. After his China achievement he had had to undergo extensive knee surgery that should have prevented him from running regularly again, yet he defied medical opinion to achieve his coastline run. In short, he's a tough guy with a strong will. Most importantly, I had built up a close friendship with him and I judged him to be someone who knows himself and who operates with integrity. He would treat me with respect, consider my opinions and understand that we were accountable to each other. Sharing the same principles and values within a team is absolutely vital to the longevity of that team and its ability to succeed; Braam and I ticked those boxes. I was sufficiently certain about him to trust him with my life, and vice versa, and I believe the personal understanding that exists between us in this regard was one of the greatest assets of our team and the reason for our success.

Just as I had done with Bill, I accepted Braam's invitation to race with him on the condition that he agreed to focus on looking after me while letting me look after him. Each person's food, hydration, health and motivation would be the responsibility of the other person. It was a winning formula that my experience with Bill had reinforced, a proactive way of easing tough team dynamics and preventing problems before they even show up.

Braam: I will never forget Pete saying to me, "Braam, I will do this race with you on one condition. You are here to look after me and I am here to look after you." And that is what we did. While preparing for our epic Antarctic expedition we grew closer as men. We shared real stories: our backgrounds, families, regrets, successes and mistakes. Our honest openness with one another has now cemented a friendship for life that is rare and deeply special. There is no competition between us, but rather collaboration.

Most professional adventurers use their expeditions to raise funds for charities or to create awareness of certain issues or initiatives. It helps to introduce a further sense of purpose to an expedition. Both Braam and I recognise that in changing one person's life you not only change their life, but also the lives of the people around them, and their communities. This is why we believe our expeditions have significance, and it is perhaps the defining idea that unites us as teammates.

Braam has always raised funds for Operation Smile, a truly uplifting international charity that provides facial reconstructive surgery to children with cleft palates and other facial deformities. The charity has provided free life-changing surgery to hundreds of thousands of children around the world. My charity of choice is the Carel du Toit Centre, which assists deaf preschool children in the Eastern Cape to learn language and speech.

Early on we also agreed to use the race to raise awareness of climate change, which was most effectively done through our unique coin-minting experience at the South Pole. Both Braam and I have become very environmentally aware and I believe we will incorporate an element of this activism in most, or even all, of our future expeditions.

The Centenary Race to the South Pole was a unique and extraordinary expedition, and the fact that Braam and I were one of only three teams that officially completed it says a huge deal both for those behind the scenes who assisted us on the way and our own relationship. Whatever you do in life, the team of people that you surround yourself with should share the same principles, values, vision and passion as you. If you are able to find such a team, then you can fly.

STONES AND MOUNTAINS
Taking small steps to achieving something epic

*"Don't be afraid to give your best to small jobs.
Every time you conquer one it makes you that
much stronger. If you do the little jobs well,
the big ones will take care of themselves."*
– Dale Carnegie

There have been many times in my life when I have faced massive challenges, whether in my personal relationships, my health or finances, at school, university, on the rugby field, at work or on my expeditions. Of course the challenges and disappointments faced by Amundsen and Scott a century ago make mine pale into insignificance, but my problems often seem insurmountable in the moment that they occur. That's just the nature of things; we all feel like this at times. If we have big goals and aspirations for our lives then we are going to face big challenges.

Often the challenges we face seem overwhelming, so much so that they can paralyse us into taking no action at all. My wife, Kim, often talks about the difficulty she faced before leaving home on her 7,000-kilometre triathlon expedition around the perimeter of South Africa. She explains how she sometimes felt immobilised by the enormity of what she had undertaken to do.

The mental process she used to deal with it all went something like this.

Nobody ever trips over mountains.

It is the stones in your path that cause you to stumble.

Navigate your way across the stones and you will find one day that you have crossed the mountain.

We have all had times in life when we are immobilised by the enormity of something we have to do: writing a difficult exam, writing a book, losing weight, getting fit and healthy, sorting out our finances, fixing a broken relationship, and so on. It is so much easier to do nothing or to procrastinate by wasting time on other things that are neither important nor urgent in comparison. Getting started, taking that first step, is often the hardest part of any challenge.

When Bill Godfrey and I started to prepare ourselves for that first row across the Atlantic in 2007, we were put in touch with Professor Tim Noakes at the Sports Science Institute in Cape Town, who would help us with various aspects of our training and diet. He suggested we make contact with a sports mind coach, David Becker, who at that stage was the legal head of the International Cricket Council based in Dubai. Initially, I didn't think getting hold of David was the most practical idea because the international distance would make any interaction we had complicated and expensive – bearing in mind we were on a seriously tight budget. We traded a few emails, but then one day out of the blue I received a phone call from Dubai.

David and I had a very interesting conversation, during which he explained that he would like to help Bill and me, free of charge. Law was his career, but being a mind coach was his passion. Given our sponsorship difficulties, we were delighted to take up the offer.

We touched on a few critical areas during our initial chat, especially the idea that both Bill and I had already accepted: that although the row would be physically very demanding, we would win or lose the race in our heads. David expanded on this by explaining that we would need to put certain processes in place if we were going to achieve our goal of winning it. Prof Noakes was right; David knew his stuff and was well worth talking to. I looked forward to our next phone call, scheduled for a week later. Seven days later, David's advice went something like this.

"Pete," he said, "today I want to chat about what I consider to be one of the most important areas you will need to focus on before and during the race. When you row out of San Sebastián at the start of the race your GPS will show 5,500 kilometres to row to your destination point. You need to change that. Although you will not consciously think about it, your mind will be telling you that that's simply too far. You need to break down the whole race and your training into bite-sized chunks. When you plan your route, you need to put waypoints into your GPS at every 150-kilometre mark and row for those marks – then when you get to each one you can reward yourself with something, anything. This will give you real, tangible targets, something that you can comprehend as being within your reach, and something to look forward to."

I immediately saw the value in what David was suggesting, and I quickly adopted this way of thinking to the endurance phase of our training. I set myself modest targets and then rewarded myself once I had achieved them. During that first row Bill and I followed David's advice, setting waypoints at intervals of 100 nautical miles. Those targets came and went, and before we knew it they just seemed to be flying past. It became far easier to focus on the small but important things in front of us (the "stones"), and in so doing complete the enormous task we'd undertaken ("crossing the mountain").

When Braam and I raced across Antarctica, our strategy was much the same. Our total distance was enormous – it would ultimately be 888 kilometres, according to our GPS – and we needed to break it down to get our heads around it. We would set a daily target, usually about 30 or 35 kilometres, depending on the weather and ice conditions, and completely ignore the overwhelming larger figure. We discussed this before the start of the race and we were clear that we would ski every day with our entire focus on the target of finishing just that one day. One step at a time, one kilometre at a time, one day at a time – that was our thinking.

That mindset was incorporated into our routine. Each small element of our routine, which was soon to become so familiar, was one small step to finishing the day in question. As we would roll up the tent every morning before starting the day's trekking, we would look at each other and say, "Just today, and in a few short hours we will be setting up the tent again." Then before we set off, particularly when the temperature was -35°C or colder, we would check each other's small "seals", the spaces between unprotected skin and clothing. It's hard to see your own face and feeling for the gaps doesn't work, so we had to check each other and make the necessary adjustments. The routine helped us avoid serious frostbite, and it also helped us to move along one step at a time.

If our hands got cold while we were trekking we would swing them fast in big circles to get the blood to the tips – again, this was part of our daily routine. We constantly needed to look after every aspect of our bodies so that they did not break down beyond repair – stepping over small stone after small stone.

Two days into the race I started to feel a bit light-headed at times and my face began to swell up. At first I didn't know what was happening and I suspected it may be from a lack of sleep. But when I chatted to Prof Noakes about it during one of our scheduled satellite phone calls, he explained that I was showing signs associated with altitude sickness. My body was obviously taking a while to adjust, and I needed to monitor the situation carefully. It was a potentially worrying diagnosis.

At the same time, Braam's chest was taking him to hell and back every day. His incessant cough was debilitating, especially at "night" when we were supposed to be resting. It was so bad at one point that, when Prof Noakes informed Braam his condition could be life-threatening given our levels of physical exertion, we seriously had to consider pulling out of the race on medical grounds. But Braam refused to let it beat him. For some strange reason he seemed to be okay while we were trekking, but as soon as we stopped moving and got into the tent the coughing would start up again with a vengeance. This meant many sleepless nights, a recipe for disaster when your body is being pushed to the limits.

Braam: In the early stages of the race proper, my coughing got really bad. I had full-blown bronchitis, if not pneumonia. After three nights of no sleep, constantly coughing and bringing up loads of muck, I was so tired I doubted for the first time if I could finish the race. Indeed, I realised there was a very real chance I could die. I was on a second course of heavy-dose antibiotics as well as cortisone, yet I still got worse. I knew Pete was really worried about me but diplomatically downplayed things with positive words of encouragement.

After my third night of no sleep, Pete suggested we stay in the tent and rest a day. It felt like a wonderful idea. When it was our scheduled time to get going, I lay in my warm sleeping bag feeling miserable but glad for the agreed-upon rest. Then it hit me. "If we don't get up now and go, I will lose the will to succeed," I realised. Pete was worried but I convinced him to go. We did a shorter day, only 24km, but during this make-or-break day I spent all my time convincing myself that I could heal. "From today, I am beginning to heal," I said, over and over and over. And that was the beginning of my recovery.

As it turned out, had we rested that day we would never have made the cutoff and would have been disqualified.

Braam's feet were another area of concern for both of us. He had a badly ingrown nail on his big toe that was agonising. Preparing his feet every morning and medicating them every evening took an age, but we simply had to get that right because an immobile Braam meant our race was over.

My altitude sickness and Braam's bronchitis-related cough and toe worries were all small problems that had to be focused on and resolved one at a time. Together they were a disaster; one by one they were manageable. Prof Noakes's medical advice helped me through the altitude sickness and in time the swelling disappeared. Braam and I adjusted our routine to incorporate more time for him to deal with his chest and feet; to save time I would set up the stoves and make water and food while Braam sorted out his feet and medicated his chest. He managed to keep his toes in check and in time his chest improved. It was amazing to see Braam push himself every day. He said to me on many occasions, "Pete, this is just a case of mind over matter. I know I'm going to get better. I did the same thing on the Great Wall of China and I can do it here!" And he did.

Together we stepped over each stone in our path and carried on trekking.

One of the rewards we gave ourselves on the last night of the race was what we called "the final supper". Physically, the last few days were as tough as anything I've had to deal with because of the added distances we had to cover to make the revised cutoff and the mental pressure that came with them. We were in high spirits working together with the Centrepoint team, but we needed further motivation to get us by. The final supper, we decided, would take place in our tent with our new British teammates. We would get all our food together and make the best meal of the race, sharing time together and chatting about the race and our various adventure stories. It was exactly what we needed to inspire us over the last small stones – actually quite big stones! – of the last few days.

I often think about how it must have felt for Scott and his team to arrive at the South Pole so physically depleted after weeks out on the ice. Frostbitten, cold and hungry, and devastated at being beaten by the Norwegians. It has even been suggested that the morale blow he and his men suffered on discovering that Amundsen had beaten them may well have been the difference between them making it back or not; I can believe it. So many small things went against Scott and his team (many beyond their powers to change) that avoiding just one or two of them along the way may have saved them.

Braam and I experienced really cold days during the last 200 kilometres of our race. As our Icelandic trainers had warned us, -25°C has nothing on -45°C! We had known we could not win the race, but that was not our intention. We made it to the final supper with Andrew, Ben and Jason and then we made it to the finish line just in time. There was elation rather than disappointment when we reached the South Pole, and then only a few hours later we were flying back over the path we had trekked for six weeks.

There were no more stones to step over; we had crossed our mountain and conquered our Eighth Summit.

A SECOND SAD POSTSCRIPT

As with the *Gquma Challenger* story, our Antarctic tale has a tragic postscript. In this case, one of the talented crew who came down to Antarctica to film us, the acclaimed photographer and cinematographer Paul van Schalkwyk has since died. Aged 58, he was killed on 8 March 2014 in a light-aircraft crash near the Etosha National Park in Namibia.

From Danie Ferreira, CEO of Urban Brew Studios:

For as long as I've known Paul, each and every day of his life he had to do two things he absolutely loathed. The one was going to bed... and the other was getting out of bed. I've always looked up to Paul as a refined fellow with numerous interests and an endearing love for life. When you grow old and you are passionate about what you do, living life becomes a race against time. Paul was always busy, and after his cancer scare four years ago, he was acutely aware of the limited remaining window he had wherein he could experience the collective joy of three of his passions – photography, flying and his love for nature.

Paul, your full life came at a great cost... especially to the ones you left behind. I cannot help but feel your tragic passing is a life interrupted, not an end to a life. You were a wise man; I've always relied on you as a friend and drew on your advice for most of my professional life. Again I find myself needing you now, in the same way you have been there for me the past 26 years – as my comrade and as my friend. Thank you for what we shared, for what you have given me; your wisdom reflects a soul that's roamed this continent for many years; your humanity and passion are an agonising loss to all.

On Saturday the 8th of March, Paul went west... for an eternal golden hour.

CONCLUSION

"I count him braver who overcomes his desires
than him who conquers his enemies;
for the hardest victory is over self."
– Aristotle

The great lessons that I have learnt from the expeditions described in this book resonate through everything we do in life.

- We are all incredibly constructed beings with enormous potential.

- Although we need to be physically prepared for whatever we do in life, the battle to succeed and to make our dreams and visions a reality – whether at work, at home or on the playing field – is not so much a physical battle as one that happens in our heads.

- With the right processes in place we can achieve so much more than we might think we're capable of; we can conquer the Eighth Summit; "the impossible" can become possible.

My first rowing race across the Atlantic Ocean, with Bill Godfrey on *Gquma Challenger*, changed my life forever. It shook my world and turned it all around. I recall rowing out of La Gomera and looking back over my shoulder at the great expanse of water that lay between us and Antigua. It was just so vast. Before I'd started preparing for the race, I had limited myself to believing that I was only capable of certain things; I was capable of attaining what I could see in front of me, not what was beyond the horizon. I had limited myself up to this point in my life because this was the "safe" thing to do, a natural self-defence. But really I had imprisoned myself with my own beliefs and prevented myself from achieving my full potential. With Bill, I discovered that our potential was like the ocean we were about to row: vast and out of sight.

That adventure, and all those that have followed, also taught me about the importance of mind over matter. Had we not started out with the overpowering drive to win the Atlantic Rowing Race, I am not sure we would have been able to do so. The six hours that separated us from the second-placed team was a mental difference that we achieved long before the start. We won the race when we decided that we were going to win it.

The solo row on *Nyamezela* allowed me a huge amount of time to reflect on my life, especially in that epic storm in the middle of the Atlantic with Simon the storm petrel by my side. I suppose that most of us are the same; perhaps it's human nature that we only take a long, hard look at ourselves and the meaning of our lives when we are alone in unfamiliar territory and facing huge adversity, possibly even death. On my own on the ocean, I could comprehend the great value of the gift we have all been given. I also realised that, if everything we ever possessed was taken away from us, the one thing that we will always have control over is our minds.

The Centenary Race to the South Pole drove home these and other lessons, and I'm sure my future expeditions will do the same. We are all involved in our own adventures or endurance events in some or other way. Human history is full of people who have lived on the edge, willing to take on life-and-death adventures. But risk is not limited to acts of physical danger. Whether you're starting a business or moving home or having a baby, you're taking a risk. *Life* is a risk!

Every great venture in life demands clear vision and dynamic strategy, precise planning and preparation, absolute honesty, integrity and uprightness of character and, above all, *perseverance*. If we persevere to our fullest capacity in the pursuit of our dreams, we absolutely *will not fail.*

So I would like to encourage you, the reader, to set up the processes in your life that will allow you to conquer your own Eighth Summit. Set clear and achievable goals, knowing that with the right resources there is a solution to every problem.

Surround yourself with the best possible team – those who share your vision and passion. Prepare yourself properly and do not be paralysed by the fear of failure. Laugh at it rather. Have a clear, but flexible strategy and be decisive. Value self-discipline. Be innovative by always looking for areas to improve upon. Understand the benefit of helping others succeed. And, finally, once you have a grand ambition in place, a mountain to climb, focus on the small important things right in front of you; your progress will be inevitable and you will get there by conquering the Eighth Summit.

GLOSSARY

Autohelm: automated system for holding a boat on course without it being manually navigated.

Automatic Identification System (AIS): automated system that continuously tracks and identifies nearby ships by electronically exchanging data.

Bow: the front part of a boat.

Dankie Tannie pakkies: bags filled with snacks and treats; from the name for bags given to South African soldiers going to the border. (Literally "Thank you Auntie packets".)

Drogue chute or drogue anchor: windsock-shaped underwater parachute of varying diameter, usually deployed from the stern of the boat, to stabilise it in rough conditions when the wind is coming from behind; specifically used to keep the back of the boat into the swell.

Emergency Position-Indicating Radio Beacon (EPIRB): a tracking transmitter used to find ships, aircraft and people in dire emergencies; distress signals are sent when manually activated or when the device is immersed in water.

Frostbite/frostnip: frostbite is the medical condition where localised damage is caused to skin and other tissue due to sub-zero temperatures; it is most likely to happen in body parts farthest from the heart and those with large exposed areas. The initial stages of frostbite are sometimes called "frostnip".

Knot (kt): unit of speed used by ships and of wind; equal to one nautical mile per hour or 1.85km/h.

Nautical mile (nm): unit of length used for navigation; equivalent to the average length of one hundredth of a degree: standardised as 1.85 kilometres or 1.15 miles.

Parachute anchor or para-anchor: a 3-metre underwater parachute deployed on a long line off the bow of the boat to minimise it being blown in the wrong direction by head and side winds; intended to act like a normal anchor and stop the boat completely, but there is usually still some drift in the direction of the current.
Pitch and roll: respectively front-to-back and side-to-side movements of a boat on the water.
Pulk: light fibreglass sledge designed to be hauled by a person.
Stern: the rear part of a boat.
VHF radio: very high frequency radio, used for close-range vessel-to-vessel communication at sea; depending on antenna size and weather conditions, range can vary widely, from 5 to 60 nautical miles.

NOTE ON UNITS OF DISTANCE AND SPEED
Measuring distances across different surface types and eras inevitably results in a confusion of unit types. Mile, nautical mile and kilometre are all used throughout the book: mile for historical authenticity or atmosphere; nautical mile because it remains the unit of maritime measurement; and kilometre for reference to make sense of the numbers when needed. Similarly, speeds indicated in knots or km/h indicate maritime or land measurements respectively.
Easy reference:
1 mile = 1.61 kilometres
1 nautical mile = 1.85 kilometres
1 knot = 1.85km/h

ACKNOWLEDGEMENTS

The Eighth Summit and the stories in it could not have been written without the assistance of many individuals.

From a production point of view, the first obvious thank you goes to all those who have generously offered their writing snippets, photographs and advice, all of which has enhanced my material no end. The cooperation I have had from people both at home and around the world in this regard has been wonderful and is hugely appreciated. To the writers of the various emails, blogs and books that have been referenced, we have occasionally altered grammar and spelling for sense and consistency; I hope you don't mind.

My profound thanks also go to Amy Smith, whose wonderful maps illustrate the three expeditions; and to Tim Richman, my editor, and his team at Burnet Media for the very obvious passion and dedication they have shown for this book. And to those at Jacana Media for their efforts in marketing and distribution.

I have dedicated this book to my beautiful wife Kim and could fill many pages with all the reasons why she inspires me every day of my life – but at this point I need to acknowledge how much time she put into helping me write this book, from making sense of it all to correcting my spelling and grammar. Thank you, Kim. *The Eighth Summit* would not have happened without your assistance and boundless energy!

To Hannah, my next greatest adventure.

To God, for showing me that we have been incredibly made and that all things are possible with Him.

To my late mother, Moira... I miss you daily, Mom. You had the greatest sense of adventure of all!

ACKNOWLEDGEMENTS

To my father, Rik. Thanks, Dad, for dedicating your life to making ours better.

To all my family – brothers, sisters, uncles and aunts – who have honed that spirit of adventure in me over the years.

To my uncles, Lionel and John Donnelly, who got the ball rolling by paying the entry fee for the first Atlantic Rowing Race.

To "Team Pete": Cliffy Coombe & Tracey Whitelaw, Tjaart van der Walt, Nic "Moose" Good, Danie Ferreira and all the key players in the book, for your ongoing friendship and assistance, particularly during my solo row. I look forward to many more adventures with you in the future.

To James Mallinson, Dylan Rankin and Morgan Johnston for creating the title songs for both row documentaries.

To Bill and Braam, my partners on the first Atlantic row and the race to the South Pole, respectively. It was an honour – and thank you for the photographs!

To all my friends and supporters, thanks for being part of my journeys and assisting Kim during my extended absences.

Unfortunately I don't have a trust fund to pay for all my adventures, so I must thank all my sponsors who have trusted me with their brands for the opportunities they have given me; without their backing there would be no stories for me to tell.

Lastly to you, the reader, thank you for choosing this book. I hope that it will have a lasting effect on your life and those around you.

Peter van Kets
May 2014

www.petervankets.com

Twitter @PetervanKets

Facebook peter.vankets.3